UNDERSTANDING
REINCARNATION

UNDERSTANDING REINCARNATION

Effective Techniques for Investigating Your
Past Lives

by

J. H. Brennan

THE AQUARIAN PRESS

This edition 1990
First published as *Five Keys to Past Lives* 1971

British Library Cataloguing in Publication Data

Brennan, J. H. (James Herbert)
Understanding Reincarnation
1. Reincarnation
I. Title.
291. 237

ISBN 1-85538-011-0

*The Aquarian Press is part of the Thorsons Publishing
Group, Wellingborough, Northamptonshire, NN8 2RQ,
England.*

Printed in Great Britain by William Collins, Sons & Co. Ltd,
Glasgow

1 3 5 7 9 10 8 6 4 2

CONTENTS

PART ONE

BACKGROUND THEORY

CHAPTER ONE

SECRET MEMORIES

Transmigration of souls, sometimes called metempsychosis, is based on the idea that a soul may pass out of one body and reside in another ... The idea appears in various forms in tribal cultures in many parts of the world (for example, Africa, Madagascar, Oceania, and South America). The notion was familiar in ancient Greece, notably in Orphism, and was adopted in a philosophical form by Plato and the Pythagoreans. The belief gained some currency in gnostic and occult forms of Christianity and Judaism and was introduced into Renaissance thought by the recovery of the Hermetic books.

Academic American Encyclopedia

I do not propose to argue any case for reincarnation in this book. Although the doctrine is accepted by half the world's major religions — and may have been accepted by early

Christianity — there is no way you can be sure it is true. Even the strictest scientific investigation of a given case can only prove the possibility of reincarnation *in that case*. Reincarnation as a general fact of life may lie beyond proof altogether. That does not mean — as many have concluded — that you are forever banned from discovering if you have lived before. At an individual level, reincarnation may be less a question of faith than of *experience*. This requires a little explanation.

As Sigmund Freud developed his theory and practice of psychiatry in Vienna, he discovered that many emotional problems were rooted in the long-forgotten experiences of childhood. He created his famous psychoanalytical method to help patients recall them. His followers added their own techniques, like hypnosis and narco-analysis, but all had the same broad aim: to *regress* patients back to early days and help them to remember.

At first, psychiatric regressions of this type stopped at childhood. But then an enthusiastic practitioner decided to find out if it was possible to regress someone beyond the point of birth. Soon patients were reporting memories of experiences within the womb. Eventually, perhaps inevitably, the ultimate jump was made. Patients were experimentally regressed *beyond* the womb. Surprisingly, they reported recollections of what appeared to be past lives.

Psychiatrists quickly abandoned 'past life' regressions as altogether too controversial for their essentially conservative profession. The material collected was dismissed as fantasy and the whole sorry episode filed away as an unimportant aberration of the human mind. There were even suggestions that pseudo-memories of this type were rare, perhaps confined to especially creative patients.

Universal Memories

As it happens, I can give the lie to that last notion from personal experience. Over three decades, I have conducted more regression experiments than I care to remember and if one thing has emerged, it is that apparent memories of past lives are almost universal.

This is something of a mystery in itself. If the material is fantasy, the question arises as to why the fantasy takes this particular form. We are not dealing with subjects whose religious convictions predispose them to a belief in reincarnation. Much of the work has been carried out with Westerners, heirs to a Judeo-Christian culture which looks forward to Heaven rather than rebirth. All seem to remember past lives. Even atheists with no belief in survival after death seem to remember past lives.

In the face of this experience, I can confidently predict there is a likelihood (which I personally believe to be approaching certainty) that there are whole histories of past lives locked inside *your* skull. Once you learn the techniques of tapping into them, they will emerge as richly detailed as any novel.

There is, of course, the possibility that this is exactly what they are — works of fiction lurking in the depths of your mind. But while much of the material unearthed during my researches did indeed bear the stamp of fantasy, some of it contained accurate historical information, often of a type which the subject was unlikely to know. This again is by no means rare, although it does not, as too many people claim, prove the memories to be genuine.

Sceptics still manage to dismiss even those cases on the grounds that subjects may simply be regurgitating books they have read or conversations they have overheard and subsequently forgotten. This is an impossible objection to answer since it relies on the fact that the mechanism which produces the material is unconscious — and as Carl Jung once pointed out, the unconscious *really is* unconscious: by definition, you are unaware of what you are doing.

Worse still, the objection is valid. People do resurrect material they have read and present it as past life recall. In one well documented case, a woman produced vivid recall of a life in ancient Rome with an impressive wealth of detail and substantial accuracy in portraying the period. Years later, investigators discovered the novel (long out of print) from which she had unconsciously drawn the story, complete with the names of Roman husband, sisters and lover.

But is *some* of the material locked in your mind may be fiction, it would be a gross error to assume *all* of it is fiction. The same woman who 'remembered' life in ancient Rome produced equally detailed memories of a life as a Jew in medieval York. This material included reference to a church crypt in which she had hidden to escape the pogroms. When the material was first published, no such crypt was known to exist. Only afterwards was it discovered by workmen engaged in renovations. Prior to this point, it had been sealed, lost and forgotten for centuries.

Dr Arthur Guirdham, formerly Chief Psychiatrist for Bath, had one patient who remembered a past life as a Cathar in France. At the time very little was known about this sect, and several details given by the woman were held by historians to be inaccurate. Research over the following decade, however, soon established that the woman's memory was right and the historians wrong: the details she had given were verified by subsequent discoveries.

It is difficult to see how this sort of data can be dismissed as fantasy or the unconscious dramatization of books once read and long forgotten. The picture that then emerges is fascinating. It would appear that, buried deep within your mind, is a body of material which presents itself as memories of your prior incarnations. This material is there (at least in my experience) whether or not you have any conscious belief in reincarnation.

Some of the material is likely to be fantasy, perhaps generated by the mechanism of wish-fulfilment or as an attempt to compensate for present-day shortcomings, or perhaps from a desire to enlarge the horizons of your personal philosophy. Some of the material is likely to be fiction, created by an unconscious mechanism which takes books you have read, movies you have seen and conversations you have listened to, and weaves them into a convincing creation which can include many instances of historical accuracy.

Genuine Memories

There is a portion of the material, however, which does not fall into either of these categories. It is material of such impact, such accuracy, and such conviction that it appears to be no less than it purports to be: memories of lives you have lived on this planet before your present birth. It is on this basis that I have concluded that reincarnation is the most likely experience any of us might undergo after physical death. When you weed out the fantasies and the fictions, what remains seems to me sufficiently convincing to put the matter almost beyond doubt.

Consequently, I have written the remainder of this book on the premise that you are interested in examining genuine past lives via an investigation of far memories. I find the repeated use of inverted commas an irritation, and phrases like *apparent past life memories* unwieldy, so for simplicity I have pretended that each memory you unearth is genuine. It is up to you to keep in mind that nothing can be called a past life memory until you have checked it thoroughly.

The book itself is largely about how to gain access to far memories. It contains a number of basic techniques, one or more of which is almost certain to work for you, as well as some speculation on the inner structures which allow genuine reincarnations to occur.

Gaining information about possible past lives is only the first step. The next and more important step is checking out the information to the best of your ability. Some help on this score is given, too.

It perhaps goes without saying that you will never find out anything about a past life just by reading a book: even a book like this one which deals with investigative techniques. You have to put the techniques into practice — something which requires effort, patience and application. But if you do take the time and make the effort, results are virtually guaranteed, at least in the sense that certain information will emerge. Check this information with care, because only after checking can you judge how worthwhile the information may be.

CHAPTER TWO

DEATH, BIRTH AND REBIRTH

Two types of anxiety are recognized in psychoanalysis. The first type, traumatic anxiety, results from overstimulation. Events happen faster than the mind can comprehend them; this produces a feeling of crisis. Sigmund Freud believed that this feeling has a physical basis in the capacity of the nervous system and that birth throws every child into a state of traumatic anxiety. In his view, this birth trauma becomes the model for later episodes of anxiety.

Academic American Encyclopedia

There are two main problems when investigating past lives. One of them is death.

Long before you consider anything so exotic as reincarnation, it becomes fairly obvious that the mechanics of human memory are peculiar. For one thing, you tend to forget anything unpleasant.

You can test this quite simply for yourself. Cast your

mind back to childhood and think about the summers. Chances are you will remember them as fine. Ask your father or your grandfather what the weather was like when he was young. Nine times out of ten, his answer will be that it was better than it is today. But what you are listening to here is not a description of weather patterns: you are listening to a quirk of human memory, which retains the good times far more easily than the bad. The psychological function of forgetting the unpleasant is thought to help in the preservation of your sanity. It prevents you from becoming overwhelmed by the hard knocks of life. Even those who have led lives of the most dire misery will still look back on 'the good old days'. The bad old days have gradually dimmed.

In cases of extreme unpleasantness, the mind will often go much further. Instead of a gradually dimming awareness, a clean break will occur. What we are talking about here is technically called *amnesia*. It enables a crisis to be quickly forgotten. An interesting example of the process if often found in people who see ghosts or undergo some similar psychical experience. Since the existence of ghosts and psychism are generally denied within our Western culture, such experiences are frequently accompanied by a sort of philosophical shock. They run contrary to the comfortable picture of reality the individual generally holds. Consequently, however dramatic and important the experiences may be, they tend to be forgotten within a few months, sometimes within a few weeks. Unfortunately, the mechanism which produces amnesia has a tendency towards overkill. It is not only the central trauma which is forgotten, but the surrounding circumstances as well. In some cases, the slate can be wiped completely clean.

Many years ago, as a newspaper reporter, I investigated a case of this type. Police discovered a well-dressed man in his middle forties lying in a ditch. He could not remember who he was, where he had come from, or how he got into his current predicament. He was taken to hospital where psychiatrists concluded he had undergone trauma — some sudden, extreme shock — which had resulted in total amnesia. The sequence, I learned, was common enough, provided the trauma was too much for the mind to bear. The man, who turned out to be a Canadian tourist, required careful treatment over several months before he could recall a single item of his former life.

What the story illustrates is not the mind's fragility, but rather one of its great strengths — a superbly efficient defence mechanism. And it is a mechanism which is of considerable importance to anyone engaged in past life research. For when you experience the greatest of all life's traumas — the moment of death — this same defence mechanism comes into play. You die, you reincarnate, but your mind blocks out the memory of your death ... and with it the memory of your whole past life.

Birth Trauma

This effect is reinforced by reincarnation's second trauma, the moment of birth. Psychologists readily recognize that birth represents a considerable shock to the infant mind, and it is not difficult to imagine why. You have enjoyed a worry-free nine months in the velvet warmth, security and comfort of your mother's womb. Then suddenly you are evicted into a terrifying world of unfamiliarity and light.

Taken together, the birth and death traumas provide a very reasonable explanation of why we do not normally have conscious recall of our previous incarnations. But the key word here is *conscious*. Amnesia, however extreme, does not destroy memories, it merely hides them away in the depths of our minds. There are several quite efficient ways to bring them out again — something we will be examining in more detail a little later.

Even the best far memories (i.e. memories of prior incarnations) are all too often incomplete. One of the most curious gaps concerns language. A typical example of this problem arose when a subject of mine recalled what appeared to be a past life in Tibet. She proved remarkably knowledgeable about the country and its customs. She was able to describe her environment and name several of her relatives and friends. *But she could not speak Tibetan.*

Sceptics claim that apparent past live memories never include the language spoken in the past life unless it happens to be a language currently familiar to the subject. This is not strictly true. A few regressed subjects have been able to use a language they had never consciously learned, but in fairness to the sceptics, such cases are rare. (I have, for example, yet to find one personally in some 30 years of research.) The question arises: why, if the memory is genuine, has the language been forgotten? Variations of this question arise in respect of skills and talents which, while remembered as features of a past life, do not always manifest in this one.

Once again, the answer lies in the nature of memory.

Throughout most of our lives, it is generally easier to remember something that happened yesterday than something that happened ten years ago. This rather obvious observation goes further than you might imagine. During the course of my education, for example, I recall that I learned the essentials of calculus. I even managed to pass one or two examinations in that subject. But I could not solve the simplest problem in calculus today. (I would have trouble solving a problem in long division.) So while I *remember* having learned calculus and can still produce a certificate or two to prove it, I no longer have the slightest recollection of the details.

The point about all this is that if I can forget calculus in the course of a few decades, how much easier is it for me to forget the learned skills of a past life lived centuries ago? The mystery is not that such things are forgotten but that so many of them — as exemplified by child prodigies, pointers among others to the reality of reincarnation — are occasionally remembered.

You will always have to put validation of a past life into its proper perspective. If it is genuine, you should be able to validate historical detail, names, dates, places and similar information. But you need not necessarily be able to do in this life what you did so easily in another.

CHAPTER THREE

SELF-DECEPTION

Most groups have status structure, or pecking order; in other words, some members have more prestige than others and exert more influence on the life of the group.

Academic American Encyclopedia

Once you start exploring your past lives, you face your second major problem — self-deception. This too springs from the basic mechanics of the human mind, as you can confirm with a little observation. Have you ever listened to a man describing how he stood up to his boss? He says he told the boss a thing or two. He says he laid down the law and didn't mince his words. He says he really put the boss into his place. Now it's possible — if only just — that all this may be true. But it isn't very likely. The interesting thing, however, is that the man wants you to believe it's true. More interesting still, he wants himself to believe it's true.

Evolutionary scientists, still convinced there are apes in our ancestral lineage, write a great deal about pack dominance amongst our cousins the chimpanzees and gorillas. It was once widely believed that the pecking order was determined by two factors alone — strength and aggression. More recent studies have unearthed a third factor which, in certain species, is vastly more important than the other two. That third factor is *display*. Status in a gorilla community, for example, is almost entirely a matter of display. The beating of the chest, the baring of the teeth, the hideous growls and terrifying charges look aggressive, but are, in the words of Diane Fawcett, a big bluff. Gorillas are among the shyest and most gentle of all Nature's creatures.

Vital Question

The question then arises: is humanity a display species or an aggressive species? The answer seems to be a bit of both, but surprisingly, display has the edge by a considerable margin. This is seen most clearly in a playground where, as youngsters strive to establish status, the air is filled with cries of 'Look at me!' 'See what I can do!' and 'Watch this!' Even in later life, status is established far more often by display than by aggression. This is why executives wear suits and more teenagers dream of becoming pop stars than boxers.

How we appear to other people is important. How we appear to ourselves is if anything even more so. So important, indeed, that most of us are quite prepared to lie — to ourselves as well as others — in order to achieve the status we seek. Dale Carnegie, that much-underrated student of human nature, has pointed out that the most vicious criminals in the United States did not see themselves as evil men. Victimized, perhaps. Misunderstood, certainly. But never evil. Carnegie was speaking of the Chicago hoodlums of the Prohibition Era, but he might just as well have used the example of Nazi Germany. The judges at the Nuremberg Trials listened patiently while the most monstrous war criminals the world had ever known tried to justify their actions and present themselves as decent, honest, kind, generous, upright and law-abiding citizens.

We all share this tendency. When you judge the actions of another, you are likely to be right. When you judge your own actions you are almost always likely to be wrong. When it comes to formulating ideas about our basic nature and importance, members of our species deceive themselves constantly. This is a very human mechanism and one that, more than almost any other factor, has contributed to general cynicism about past life recall.

The famous medium Daniel Dunglas Home once remarked, 'I have had the pleasure of meeting at least 12 Marie Antoinettes, six or seven Marys of Scotland, a whole host of Louis and other kings, about 20 Great Alexanders, but never a plain John Smith. I indeed would like to cage the latter curiosity.'

I know what he means. Anyone who, like myself, shows the slightest interest in reincarnation research soon attracts a stream of people loudly claiming they were once the Bard of Avon or the Queen of Egypt. They are seldom convincing. Their research is often confined to personal intuitions or the proclamations of some psychic. And their status in this life seems to be in inverse proportion to the status of the claimed incarnation. How can so many of today's most silly individuals have been the geniuses of yester-year? How can so many dull women be reincarnations of Cleopatra? How can so many weak men lay claim to past lives as Napoleon or Caesar? The answer, of course, is that self-deception has crept in. The fantasy of a past life among the great and powerful compensates for present-life shortcomings.

Please do not assume you are immune to this process. None of us is. A past life as Henry VIII or Queen Elizabeth I will always seem more interesting, more exciting, more important, more worthy of investigation than a past life as a beggar or a thief. Yet at any given historical period, the great and powerful will form, on average, no more than 10 per cent of the total population. Which means, statistically, you are 10 times more likely to have reincarnated as a commoner than a king.

Rule of Caution

All of which brings me to the first firm rule for using this book: *Exercise extreme caution when your last life appears alluring. Be even more suspicious if results indicate you are the reincarnation of a famous person.*

Oddly enough, past lives as a famous person are among the most difficult to validate. If I recall a past life as an obscure Victorian curate hanged for murdering his wife, and subsequently discover such an individual really existed, I have an evidential situation. If I recall a past life as Henry VIII ordering the execution of Catherine or Anne, the details provide no substantial evidence at all, simply because they are well known. It is possible, of course, that you were once Helen of Troy. But it is very unlikely. If there is no way of establishing firm historical evidence — which means recalling details not in the public domain — then it is best to forget these interesting visions altogether.

Having voiced this warning, I feel compelled to mention

the danger of swinging too far in the opposite direction. Once, during a broadcast discussion of far memory, one of the other participants voiced the criticism that those who claimed to recall past lives always seemed to have been something glamorous, like a Roman legionnaire. This is not nearly such a fair point as it appears. If I were to tell you that I had just begun a new career as a private in the British Army or an American GI, I doubt that you would consider my new life glamorous. Yet these careers are exact analogies of life as a Roman legionnaire. The only difference is historical perspective.

Some past lives do indeed appear more glamorous than their modern counterparts, but it is only distance which lends enchantment. When evaluating any far memories this book may help you revive, try to place them in perspective. Be suspicious of the glamorous, but be sure it *really is* glamorous.

CHAPTER FOUR

CASE STUDIES

Memory is the process of storing and retrieving information. While popularly regarded as a single 'faculty', human memory is more usefully considered as a whole range of processes, from those allowing the brief storage of sensory information during perception to the process underlying the retention of knowledge of a language or the recollection of a personal experience.

Academic American Encyclopedia

How does far memory manifest? There have been a large number of case studies which answer this question, and answer it in a very dramatic manner since, to gain a place in the literature, they tend to be cases where reincarnation seems to be the only reasonable explanation.

In 1929, for example, a three-year-old child in Delhi, India, began to exhibit far memories which were to make her one of the best-known reincarnation studies ever. Her name was Shanti Devi and, almost as soon as she had learned to talk, she began to tell her parents about her 'husband' and her 'children'.

Many small children have similar fantasies, so for a time Shanti's parents did not take her descriptions seriously. But they persisted and grew, if anything, more detailed. Four years later, at the age of seven, Shanti was still insisting she had a husband ... but now she named him as Kedarnath, claimed she herself was called Ludgi and insisted she had borne him three children (whom she also named and described). They had lived together in a town called Muttra, where she had died in childbirth with her fourth child, in 1925.

This was too much for her parents. Muttra actually existed — it was a smallish town some miles from Delhi. But it was Shanti's claim to have died in childbirth that was most worrying — it sounded like an obscure pathology. Eventually her parents felt compelled to consult a doctor. At this point, the case took the first of many bizarre turns. The doctor listed to the child's description of her 'death' and concluded it contained medical details which a seven-year-old could not possibly know. None of his examinations produced any evidence to suggest she was physically or mentally ill.

Then chance stepped in. A business acquaintance of Shanti's father called at the house. Shanti opened the door and recognized him at once as a cousin of her past-life husband. But this claim proved more than fantasy. The man actually lived in Muttra and had a cousin named Kedarnath. Worse still, Kedarnath had had a wife named Ludgi, who died in childbirth.

In India, reincarnation is as widely accepted as Heaven and Hell are in the West. Despite their earlier scepticism, Shanti's parents were more willing to accept the possibility their daughter could have lived before than a Western couple might have been. Without telling Shanti, they arranged a test. But when this stranger called at the door, Shanti recognized him without hesitation. She had once again met Kedarnath, the man she claimed was her husband in her previous life.

By now interest created in the case was running so high that an investigative committee was set up by the Indian government. Scientists descended to carry out a full investigation. For the first time, Shanti visited Muttra ... and proved so familiar with the town that she was able to lead the researchers through it blindfold! When the bandage was removed from her eyes, she had no trouble finding her former home, where she recognized and correctly named Kedarnath's father, mother and brother.

Kedarnath's children by his deceased wife Ludgi were brought out. Amid scenes of intense emotion, Shanti recognized three of them. The fourth, whom she did not know, was the child born as Ludgi died. Shanti Devi then took the scientists to the home of Ludgi's mother, where she proceeded to point out structural and decorative differences to the house as she remembered it. Ludgi's mother, wary though she was of this strange child with her retinue of scientists, nonetheless confirmed the changes had all taken place since Ludgi's death.

As final proof, Shanti insisted Ludgi had buried some rings before she died, and volunteered to show the investigators where they were hidden. The scientists dug where she indicated and did indeed discover a small bag of rings. Ludgi's mother identified them as having belonged to her daughter. The scientific committee eventually filed a report in which they freely admitted to having found no indications of trickery or fraud.

Reincarnated Murderer

Sometimes far memories emerge in circumstances that would do justice to a thriller movie. One well-documented case concerned a Sri Lankan man facing the death sentence for the murder of his wife. When his brother visited the prison to offer sympathy in the final hours, the killer shrugged off his predicament and predicted that he would return. Subsequent events suggested he did exactly that. The brother's wife gave birth to a son (with a withered arm) who very quickly began to show physical and psychological similarities to the dead killer. At the age of two, far memories began to surface in the child. He claimed to have murdered his wife in an earlier existence, and over a period of time began accurately to fill in details ... including a grisly memory of what it felt like to be hanged.

Bishen Chand, the son of Bareilly railway clerk Ram Ghulam Kapoor, began to experience far memory when he was five years old. The fact that something strange was happening emerged when (although he did not yet know the facts of life) he began to discuss sex with his embarrassed father, even suggesting the man should take a mistress. Bishen's memories corresponded to the life of an individual named Laxmi Narain, who had died in 1918 at the age of 32. Laxmi had had a passion for a prostitute named Padma. In a striking example of the sort of weirdness that can arise in cases of this type, Padma walked in Bishen's office at Tenakpore when he was 18 years old.

The young man was so overcome by emotion that he fainted, but that night he recovered sufficiently to go to her home, carrying a bottle of wine and determined to take up the old relationship. Padma threw him out. She said that even if he was Laxmi reincarnate, she was now old enough to be his mother.

Far memory is not, it would seem, confined to hot countries. In Alaska, the grandfather of a family of Tlingit fishermen maintained that he would reincarnate in the same family and, as a sign, manifest the same birthmarks. He gave his son his watch, remarking that he would claim it back when he returned in a new body.

The grandfather died. Within a year a son was born into the family, bearing the same birthmarks. At the age of five, he claimed the watch ...

Reincarnated Victim

A rather more recent case occurred in 1968, reminiscent of the Shanti Devi case outlined above. Here a two-year-old New Delhi child, Reena Gupta, claimed to her grandmother that she had a husband. Unlike Shanti, however, Reena claimed that her husband had murdered her.

The child's behaviour soon became bizarre. She took to searching faces in the crowd for her husband and four children. She criticized her mother for the way she did the housework, and on one occasion even wandered off in the market, following a woman she believed to have visited her home in her previous life.

Vijendra Kaur, a colleague of Reena's mother, discovered a Sikh couple whose history seemed to coincide with the stories the little girl was telling. The couple, Mr and Mrs Sardar Kishan Singh, were the parents of a woman named Gurdeep Kaur, who had been murdered by her husband on 2 June, 1961. The Singhs agreed to visit Reena's home. Reena herself was asleep when they arrived, but awoke to identify them at once as her 'father and mother'.

The following day, Gurdeep's sister Swarna was brought to the Gupta home. Reena not only recognized her, but called her by a family nickname, Sarno. Later Reena was to visit the Singh household, where she correctly identified a photograph of Gurdeep, claiming it to be a picture of herself.

Joey Verwey of Pretoria, South Africa was three years old when she first experienced far memory. Her case attracted the attention of Dr Arthur Bleksley, who was convinced by the evidence. The child, he said, had described objects, manners and fashions of past ages in such minute detail that only reincarnation could explain it.

Another three-year-old, Romy Crees, in 1981 produced graphic recollections of her life as Joe Williams, a father of three who had met his death in a motor cycle accident. Romy recalled going to school in a place called Charles City, living in a red brick house, and eventually marrying a woman by the name of Sheila. She stated that her mother's name was Louise and that she suffered from a pain or injury in her right leg.

Romy's parents called in the professional researcher Hemendra Banerjee, who decided to take Romy to Charles City, 140 miles away from her home in Des Moines, Iowa. With them went Romy's father Barry Crees, Banerjee's wife and research colleague Margit, and a specialist from Des Moines, Dr Greg States. None of them told Romy where they were going. As they approached the town she suddenly began to insist they buy her mother blue flowers and mentioned that they would not be able to enter her house through the front door, but would have to 'go round the corner to the door in the middle'.

As predicted, there was indeed a Mrs Williams living in Charles City. But when the party reached the house, they found they could not use the front door — the path was blocked by a prominent notice which required them to go round the back. Mrs Williams, a 76-year-old on crutches, confirmed that her son Joe died in a motor cycle accident near Chicago in 1975 — two years before Romy was born. The house, which was now a white bungalow, had been a red brick building when Joe was young. Joe had married a woman named Sheila and, as Romy claimed, fathered three children.

Best-Known Reincarnation

Possibly the world's best-known case of reincarnation is that of His Holiness the Dalai Lama of Tibet. Prior to the Chinese invasion of 1950, Tibet was the only reincarnatory monarchy on earth. The notion of such a system is so bizarre to Western minds that the evidence for reincarnation emerging from it has largely been ignored.

The fourteenth (and current) Dalai Lama was born into a peasant family living in the north-east Tibetan village of Takster in 1935, approximately two years after the death of the previous Dalai Lama. When this peasant boy was almost two years old, a party of dignitaries arrived in the village, guided by a series of omens, portents and visions. The purpose of the party was to discover the next incarnation of Tibet's leader. (The belief at the time was that each of the previous 13 Dalai Lamas had been the serial reincarnation of the same individual. It was a further article of faith that the first Dalai Lama was an incarnation of Chenresig, the patron god of Tibet.)

Two members of the party engaged in a subterfuge worthy of comic opera. A junior official pretended to be the leader, while the real leader, a high-born lama, dressed in poor clothes and pretended to be a servant. The little peasant boy was not deceived. He recognized and asked for a rosary belonging to the old Dalai Lama, which now hung around the lama's neck. He knew the name of the servant pretending to be leader and the origin of the leader pretending to be servant.

Later, the full party conducted a series of tests. Offered two black rosaries, the boy chose that of the old Dalai Lama and placed it around his own neck. The same thing happened in a choice between two yellow rosaries. Then came a choice of drums. On the one hand was a small drum which had belonged to the old Dalai Lama. On the other was a larger, more ornate instrument with golden straps which might be expected to appeal to a small child. But the youngster chose the small drum and began to beat out a prayer rhythm. Finally came a choice of walking sticks. Once again the child picked the item which had belonged to the old Dalai Lama.

These were simple tests, but by no means naïve. They were carried out by officials as conscious as any scientist of making absolutely certain of the validity of their findings. At the time, the office of Dalai Lama combined supreme spiritual and temporal power in the country, creating the ultimate dictatorship of bodies and souls, rather as if the president of the United States were suddenly made Pope as well. Individuals to fill such an office were selected with extreme care in a process that could — and in this case did — take years. No one relished the thought of making a mistake. This being the case, the evidence presented has to be taken seriously.

CHAPTER FIVE

PERSONAL RECALL

Mental experiences fall into natural groupings or states of consciousness. Sometimes their pattern and quality are so different from the ordinary that it is more useful to say that one is in an altered state of consciousness, such as a religious trance. Mental functioning and outward behaviour in altered states can be impaired, improved, or merely changed. Besides having possible innate value, altered states may cast light upon the organization of the ordinary mental state.

Academic American Encyclopedia

Despite their diversity, all the foregoing case histories had one thing in common: they involved spontaneous eruptions of far memory. It is a central thesis of reincarnation research that far memories can be artificially stimulated — that, in other words, we do not have to wait for their spontaneous appearance.

It is also true, however, to say that some people find it

easier to stimulate their far memories than others. It seems as if there are those among us who, while they have not yet experienced spontaneous far memory, are very ripe to do so. Sometimes it is even possible to decide whether you might be one of them, by carefully searching out the signs. Have you, for example, found yourself strangely drawn towards a particular country without really knowing why? Do you have a fascination for a particular style (or period) of furniture? Do you enjoy movies set in a particular historical period? All these things *may* be indications of a past life in that country or during that period. Feelings of this type can be a result of far memories pushing towards the surface of your consciousness.

An even more striking example of the same psychological dynamic is the recurring dream. Several years ago, a colleague of mine recounted a vivid dream in which she was walking across a small amphitheatre, cheered on by an enthusiastic crowd. In the dream she felt extremely ill, but recognized it was important to reach the other side. She did not manage to do so, however, and the dream ended as she sank down dying on the sand. The woman concerned did not (at that time) believe in reincarnation and was interested in the dream only in so far as a) it had recurred at intervals over a period of more than 20 years, and b) why she should have such a dream at all. Her description of the amphitheatre, the crowd and her clothing all suggested ancient Greece or Rome, but the woman herself was not a Classics scholar — her educational background and career were scientific — and she had no particular interest in either country.

Hypnotic investigation subsequently unearthed a far memory relating to a Mediterranean country (which no longer exists) called Lycia, with the arena incident an important aspect of the past life recalled. Once the complete far memory became conscious, the woman ceased to have the recurring dream, as if it had merely been her unconscious mind trying to draw her attention to the life in question.

Even if you have no indication at all of what your past lives may have been, the techniques given in this book are still likely to stimulate the sort of information you are looking for. Before you use them, however, it is as well to have some idea of what you are heading into.

The Nature of Far Memory

Not long ago, while organizing a seminar on reincarnation research, I mentioned to the Conference Centre manager that I planned to demonstrate regression techniques to those attending. 'I suppose you *do* have ways to bring them back?' she asked me anxiously. Amusing though it was, the question illustrated the type of misconception people can have about the nature of the far memory experience.

The first and most important thing to remember is that every technique in this book — and every other reincarnation research technique I have ever come across, for that matter — involves the stimulation of far *memory*. None involves time travel, as my Conference Centre manager obviously believed. But her question was not nearly so naïve as it might appear. There are at least two techniques which can generate perceptions so vivid that you might be forgiven for believing time travel really *was* involved. These techniques are hypnosis and the Christos Method. We will be examining both in more detail a little later. For the moment, all I want to do is point out that for certain subjects (not all subjects, but a fairly sizeable minority) both hypnosis and Christos can give a powerful subjective impression of not just remembering a past life, but of actually reliving it. This can create problems.

On one occasion, for example, I was using the Christos Method to stimulate far memory in the mayor of a northern English town. Although Christos does not involve trance, the mayor's experience grew progressively more vivid as the session continued. Eventually she reached an area of memory which involved recall of crossing a narrow ledge with a steep drop on either side. In the middle of her description of this experience, she began, quite suddenly, to sweat and shake. The colour drained from her face. I thought she had taken ill and asked her what was the matter. She told me she was afraid of falling. I reminded her that falling in her present situation was impossible (she was lying on the floor of my study at the time), and invited her to open her eyes. She did so and relaxed at once. All that was needed was a reminder of where she really was. But her *subjective* experience up to that point had clearly been one of standing on the ledge.

The problem with this type of thing is not, as the Conference Centre manager imagined, bringing a subject 'back'. Where the real trouble lies is that such vivid recall can stimulate a process known to psychiatrists as *abreaction*, the abrupt, often violent discharge of emotion related to a traumatic experience. It occurs in psychoanalysis and similar techniques when the root cause of a neurosis is finally discovered, and is essential to successful therapy. But abreaction is safe only when the ground has been carefully prepared, when, that is, the patient is ready to handle the emotion involved. If the patient is *not* prepared, abreaction, which is always painful, may become totally unmanageable, and may lead to a complete breakdown.

I have no wish to frighten you away from the investigation of your past lives, but the fact remains that far memory can involve abreaction to some degree. One subject I worked with experienced emotional turmoil for almost six months following an upsurge of distant memory. Another found herself on the edge of suicide. Extreme reactions of this type are, fortunately, rare, the essential difference between psychiatric and far memory abreactions being that those who experience the former are, by definition, suffering from some form of emotional or mental stress (otherwise they would not be getting psychiatric treatment), while those experiencing the latter, by and large, are not. Nonetheless, far memory of any sort can be disturbing, and vivid far memory, where past-life experiences are subjectively relived, can sometimes be very disturbing indeed. For this reason, it is a good rule of thumb not to undertake reincarnation research (on your own past lives at any rate) while you are suffering from any serious emotional or physical illness. The experience may prove a strain, and is consequently better undertaken when you are fit and well.

CHAPTER SIX

USING THIS BOOK

Experimental research requires that the experimenter
manipulate the conditions of the research as they
affect the subject: for example, presenting several
stimulus conditions or a series of learning trials.
Experimental research contrasts to naturalistic, or
observational, research, in which the investigator
observes events as a passive outsider and has little or
no systematic control over them.

Academic American Encyclopedia

Broadly speaking, there is only one way to obtain detailed information about your past lives, and that is to remember them. Most of the techniques in this book are aimed towards that end, towards gently circumventing the traumatic barriers of death and birth. Indeed, I am increasingly tempted to believe that — although it may not appear so on the surface — *all* the techniques given tap into the far memory experience, a point we will return to when we examine the techniques themselves.

Not every method will work for you. If there was a single road for everyone, I could have saved myself a lot of time and trouble both in writing and research. So read through the whole book first — it is quite short and will not take up too much of your time — before you are tempted to put any particular technique into practice. Then, when you have an idea of the overall picture, select your method. Which one you start with is largely a matter of taste. Often your intuition will lead you quickly to the one most suited to your temperament.

By reading through, you will discover the systems fall into two distinct categories. Some present a broad overview of your past lives, others concentrate on filling in the details. Generally speaking, the former category is a little easier for the beginner, but here again you must decide what you want and select accordingly. Once you have chosen your method, set aside some serious time to try it out. Not everything works well — or even works at all — first time. This is especially true of advanced techniques like hypnosis. One of my best subjects, a Zambian businessman, initially proved so difficult to hypnotize that I was fast coming to the conclusion he was immune to induction. Then, over the course of a single evening, he fell into a trance so deep he was able to open his eyes without influencing his state.

Check Your Results

As in most things, perseverance makes a great deal of difference to the results of reincarnation research. Never give up on any method until you have tried it at least five times. And if a given technique *really* brings no worthwhile results after several attempts, move on to another. It is very unlikely indeed that you will fail to get results from *all* of the methods given. Once you do achieve results, never lose sight of the fact that you must mistrust all information obtained. This is particularly true of information which comes through hypnotic regressions or Christos visions, which are often so fascinating in themselves that they positively command belief. But however obtained, every item of data should be double-checked where possible.

I cannot stress that last point strongly enough. Should you find, for instance, that you were a sixteenth-century Spanish peasant in your past life, go to your local library and borrow everything you can about the period. Check the details of your visions against the facts and, if the visions fail to measure up, forget them. Incidentally, it is as well to do your checking *after* you have made a careful note of the details of your far memories. We have already examined the mechanics of self-deception, and your unconscious mind is quite capable of representing historical research as if it were far memory.

Even if your unconscious decides to behave itself, checking out a particular country or historical period in advance will always tend to invalidate the evidential value of your memories. In one regression experiment, a subject of mine recalled a singularly unpleasant incarnation as a known Nazi war criminal notorious for her delight in using the skins of gas chamber victims to cover lampshades. Although the far memory was detailed, it was not particularly evidential since my subject, a writer by profession, had been researching the Nazi period for several years as part of a book she was writing on the part played by women in the Holocaust. The material she produced during our regression sessions *might* have been genuine far memories, but there was simply no way to be certain.

While you can guard against this by carefully documenting your far memory as much as possible before setting out to check historical facts, even a sensible approach of this type is no guarantee that you will be able to validate the material. One of my favourite regression subjects, Pan Collins, having recalled details of a life as a woman named Cynthia Lambert in the late eighteenth and early nineteenth centuries, brought all her considerable talents as a professional researcher to bear on checking the historical validity of her memories. She was unable to do so. Although there were records of a Lambert family in the right time and place, the male chauvinistic culture of the period was extremely tardy in recording information on female members of the line. The case had to be abandoned as, at best, unproven.

There may, of course, be times when it is obviously worthless even to attempt an historical check. You might, for example, recall a past life in pre-history where records, by definition, do not exist and for which even the best scholarly descriptions include much guess-work. Or, worse still, you may find yourself recalling a past life in some essentially controversial setting like the fabulous lost continent of Atlantis. (A surprisingly large number of subjects do, including many who would not give the idea of Atlantis any credence in their waking state.) When you find yourself in such a situation, a degree of checking is still possible, although you are unlikely to end up with anything approaching proof. The trick is to use the techniques you have learned to return to the same era time and time again. Compare your notes each time ... and play detective. What you are looking for is internal consistency. (Detectives grow very suspicious when somebody trying to tell the same story twice falls down on the details.)

You might also consider the liberal application of

common sense. All cultures develop in relation to their environment and in accordance with quite clearly defined laws. Put at its most crude, you would not expect to find a nation of sailors in the middle of the Sahara Desert. As you collect your data, you can decide fairly quickly whether or not the life you remember living is solidly based. You will never prove it was genuine, but applying common sense can often show if it was not.

Reincarnation Process

Validating far memories is not the only area of research open to you when you begin to use the techniques. You might, for example, decide to find out more about the reincarnation process itself. Those of us who bother to think about reincarnation at all tend to have a fairly simplistic picture of how it works. We imagine an individual soul (or mind, or personality) which flits from one body to the next as a butterfly might flit from flower to flower. Oddly enough, the Buddhist faith (which is entirely centred on reincarnation, with the ultimate goal being how to stop it) advocates a doctrine which seems, at first glance, a contradiction in terms. This is the doctrine of *anatta,* which holds that human beings have no soul. This creates a paradox, for if it is not the soul that reincarnates, what does? Some aspects of my own research suggest, with Buddhism, that the answer may be ... nothing. But the paradox resolves itself once we realize there is a flaw in our perception not only of the reincarnation process but in the way we think about the inner structure of human beings.

The picture built up from my own research is that before you ever did anything at all in the way of (re)incarnation, you existed as a sort of Oversoul, on a dimension different to the one you are aware of now. This Oversoul did not incarnate, but rather reached into the world of matter and there built a personality which did, in fact, incarnate. This personality was not the Oversoul, which remained in its own dimension. Rather, the personality became a vehicle by means of which the Oversoul could investigate, experience and examine matter via its intimate linkage with a physical body. At the end of the life of the physical body, the personality was withdrawn and absorbed back into the Oversoul, incorporating in the Oversoul the experiences the personality had undergone. After a time, the Oversoul reached into the world of matter again and created another personality which linked with another body. And so on, over a chain of lives.

It is evident from this picture that nothing permanent incarnates. The Oversoul does not incarnate at all and each individual personality is withdrawn and absorbed at death. But at the same time, there is an obvious connection between the various lives that make up this peculiar daisy-chain — the fact that they are all lives associated with the same Oversoul. If any difficulty arises out of all this, it is the difficulty of viewpoint. We tend to look at things from the viewpoint of the (current) incarnating personality — since that is what we are — while the process only becomes clear if seen from the viewpoint of the Oversoul.

I am not, as it happens, the only one to have hit on the idea of an Oversoul. Essentially the same concept has appeared more than once in mystical literature. This does not, of course, make it true, but it does suggest that the *experience* of an Oversoul is a fairly common aspect of the human mind. It is areas like this which make reincarnation research such an interesting undertaking — one in which you can now join by using the techniques that follow.

PART TWO

THE TECHNIQUES

CHAPTER SEVEN

THE OUIJA BOARD

Automatic writing is writing produced while a person is unconscious or semiconscious of the act. In the nineteenth century the phenomenon was used by practitioners of Spiritualism, who sometimes employed devices such as the ouija board ...

Academic American Encyclopedia

The name 'ouija' derives from the French word *oui*, meaning 'yes' and the German *ja*, which also means 'yes'. Together they suggest, quite correctly, that the device is designed to answer questions.

At its most sophisticated, a ouija is a heart-shaped wooden board fitted with ball-bearings on the bottom. When placed on a flat surface, this arrangement allows it to move freely in any direction. Ideally, the surface should be polished to cut friction to a minimum. The board is used in conjunction with the letters of the alphabet, printed on cards — a Lexicon pack is perfect — on tiles from a game of Scrabble, or simply written on scraps of paper and arranged in a circle around the table. It is a good idea to include the words *Yes* and *No,* set into the left and right of the circle respectively. For convenience, you may also like to add the numbers 0 to 9.

When I first began to take an interest in psychical research, ouija boards were next to impossible to buy. They had enjoyed something of a heyday in Victorian times, then fallen into a total decline so that only the most specialized of specialist suppliers could supply them. All that has changed now. There are a great many vendors of esoteric equipment up and down the country, and ouija boards have grown so popular that they have even been offered to a general market as an entertaining novelty.

You should not allow yourself to be influenced by this sort of frivolity. Properly handled, the ouija works and the results you can obtain from it go a lot further than parlour games. If cash is in short supply or you genuinely cannot find a ouija on sale anywhere, you should not find it all that difficult to make one. Begin by drawing a heart shape (which should be a little larger than your hand) on a suitable piece of board. Plywood works fine, or, if you prefer something more substantial, any easily worked wood (no more than half an inch thick) will do.

Cut around the shape you have drawn using a jigsaw or similar tool, then sand the whole thing smooth. If you have

an artistic turn of mind, you might enjoy decorating the board, but even if you haven't, it is quite a good idea to highlight the tip of the heart in black or white. When you have finished, seal the board with a clear polyurethane-based varnish.

Adding ball-bearings is a job for a specialist — at least I have never been able to manage it — but small castors, available from any hardware store, will be just as effective. You will need three in total. Make sure they move freely and swivel cleanly in all directions. Buy the smallest you can find.

Place castors as shown

Attach the castors to the bottom of your board in a triangular formation as shown, with the apex of the triangle about two inches back from the point of the heart. Once the castors have been screwed on, you will be left with a board that is very stable to handle, yet moves freely in all directions.

Using a ouija is simplicity itself. First lay out the letters in a circle round the table, then place the ouija board in the middle. Next place the fingers of your right hand *lightly* on the upper surface of the board. Try to relax as much as possible, and wait. Waiting can actually be the toughest part of the whole operation. It may take anything up to 20 minutes. Or, indeed, you may have to make more than one attempt before anything of interest happens. Unless you are very unlucky, however, something *will* happen. The ouija will begin to move, as if of its own accord. This is just the first step, but it is by far the most important one. Give it time to happen and don't try to force it. The best attitude is one of calm confidence. Adopt it with patience and you will rarely fail to get results.

It is a very weird sensation when the board begins to move. The first time it happens, you are likely to tense up at once — which will probably ensure the board stops moving right away. But all you need do is relax and, with any luck, the movement will start up again very quickly.

Ouija Movement

It is important to note that the board will move *of its own accord*. You do not push it around, however gently. Nor do you *will* it to move — indeed, the whole thing works best if you do not concentrate on it at all. A useful tip is to read a good book while your hand is resting lightly on the board, preferably an absorbing work of fiction. The most likely time for the ouija to start moving is when your mind is fully drawn into the plot.

What makes the ouija move is a matter of opinion. Spiritualists, who have made use of this and similar devices for generations, maintain it is a question of spirit guidance. A disembodied entity from the Beyond takes control of the board (or, alternatively, takes control of your hand) and gently moves it along. According to this theory, you have, by deciding to use the ouija in the first place, offered yourself as a medium for the spirit forces, and when the board moves, those forces are shown to have manifested.

The spirit intervention theory is not confined to Spiritualists. Variations on the ouija have been used for centuries in countries with such differing cultures as mainland China (where the device is known as the 'flying pencil') and nineteenth-century France. Almost without exception, spirits have been credited with influencing the board's behaviour. Modern psychology, however, takes another view. Here the consensus is that the board is not moved by spirits, whatever superficial appearances would lead you to believe, but by your own unconscious mind.

I lean towards this latter explanation myself, but with substantial reservations. Without wanting to waste your time discussing the pros and cons of a complex theory, it seems to me that *if* something in your unconscious moves the board, then that something may form a channel to the far memories we know lie hidden in the depths of your mind. But even if this is not the case, even if spirits are involved, the empirical fact remains that the ouija can deliver valid information. It does so by answering questions.

I have no doubt at all that you will feel a complete fool the first time you try this (I certainly did). It takes a rare individual to ask, 'Is anybody there?' with complete aplomb. But ask you must. Worse still, you must ask it *aloud*. Mental questions may well get answers, but the old problem of self-deception is greatly increased. Furthermore, it is my experience that the board works far faster and more effectively if you talk to it aloud.

Do not worry if at first the replies are gibberish. The ouija will typically take a little time to settle down. Before it does, you will watch it move from letter to letter as if finding its bearings, like a blind man fumbling in an unfamiliar room. Eventually it will return to a central position, as if waiting. It may even tremble a little in anticipation.

Questioning the Board

This is the time to start asking the serious questions. When you do, you may expect answers spelt out, letter by letter, as the board moves round the table. You might imagine that once you get it going this would be a straightforward process, where all you would have to do is wait and take a note of the results. But once you have passed beyond the initial excitement of watching the board move, a very common difficulty arises: the powerful temptation to guess the ending of a word and force the board in the direction of the relevant letters. It is a temptation that is remarkably difficult to resist — the same psychological dynamic that prompts you to finish sentences for a very slow speaker. But it is important that you do resist it, since it is all too easy *to* distort a message completely.

Do not ask the ouija about past incarnations on your first attempt at using it. In fact, serious questions of any sort should be avoided until you have become well accustomed to the technique. The trick is to work with the ouija until you are completely relaxed and confident, then you can move on to more interesting things.

However you feel about the Spirit v Unconscious Mind controversy, you will soon discover that whatever moves the board *behaves* like a personality. It will have its own turn of phrase, its own comments, remarks and objections. After a few sessions, you will be well able to understand why so many people consider ouija communications spirit-driven.

This may be a good point at which to face the fact that a great many people, among them notable Church leaders, consider the use of the ouija to be dangerous. The majority of those who hold this opinion subscribe to a variation of the spirit communication hypothesis which claims that the communicating entity is at best mischievous and at worst demonic. They claim that those who use the ouija run the risk of being unduly influenced by its messages, or, in extreme cases, actually possessed by the spirit behind them.

I find myself in some difficulty in dealing with this sort of objection, mainly because I feel a good many of the points made have validity. I certainly have come across people who were unduly (often stupidly) influenced by ouija messages, reacting to their content uncritically, failing to apply common sense and generally behaving as if the most crass inanities had been inscribed by God in tablets of stone. I have not yet come across a case of ouija possession, but I am quite prepared to accept that such cases have occurred. Having said all this, however, I do not believe it adds up to sufficient reason for avoiding the use of the ouija. Cases of undue influence are rare, cases of possession very rare indeed. Dangers exist, as dangers exist in crossing the road or plugging in a kettle. There are people who are unduly influenced by watching television (I may even be one of them), but this is hardly an argument for closing down the transmitter.

Safety Guidelines

The guidelines for safe ouija communication are simple: apply common sense to every message that comes through, and believe nothing until you have checked it thoroughly. When you use a ouija you are not speaking with some superhuman entity, you are talking to a total stranger who may or may not be telling you the truth.

Messages via the ouija can be impressive in their scope and content. Typically, you will find the same personality 'coming through' time and again. But this does not always happen right away. In the early stages, several different entities may manifest, sometimes even in the same sitting. This is another reason for waiting before you start to ask serious questions. Unless you are very naïve, you do not ask advice from a total stranger. Exactly the same attitude should be applied to the curious personalities of the ouija. In other words, get to know the entity you are talking to. And make up your own mind how reliable it is.

Although all this leans towards the hypothesis of spirit communication, a little thought will show you the advice holds good even if the motive force for the board arises from your own unconscious. There are elements in your psyche which, given half a chance, will feed your conscious mind a great deal of nonsense. If you are, in fact, tapping into your unconscious with the ouija, it is just as important to make sure that the channel is clear and the information accurate.

Spiritualist or psychologist, you should test the system thoroughly before using it to solve such a delicate problem as the history of your last incarnation. Since careful testing has a lot to do with the accuracy of later results, I will spend a little more time examining these early stages.

While I have already advised you to avoid serious questions, I am not trying to suggest your initial queries should be frivolous. On the contrary, a frivolous question simply asks for a frivolous answer, which tells you nothing other than that the communicating entity has a sense of humour. Aim to ask questions which require reasonable answers, but avoid life and death topics.

There seem to be two broad types of reaction to this form of communication — superstitious awe and gross inanity. Neither gets you very far. I once heard a young woman threaten suicide because the ouija predicted she would never marry. Given the problems marriage tends to generate for most women, this was a silly enough reaction in the first place. It became doubly so when, two years later, the ouija proved wrong and she walked happily down the aisle. Fortunately a suicidal degree of awe is rare, but inanity is not. I have lost count of the number of times I have winced at questions like 'What is the door number of my Aunt Rachel's house in Brighton?' If it really is spirits who provide ouija answers, I could imagine them wincing too.

It is a good idea to treat the ouija as you would a stranger — with polite interest. Eventually, as you get to know the communicating personality, you will form your own opinions of its truthfulness and judgement. At that stage, providing you are satisfied with the entity's *bona fides,* you can begin asking questions about your past incarnations. Avoid suggesting too much. You may, for all I know, strongly suspect you were once Ghengis Khan. But however strong your conviction, do not ask questions like 'Was I a Mongolian leader last time around?' In a court of law, this is known as a 'leading question', and is generally disallowed under the rules of evidence. The form of the question strongly suggests the answer. Judges are not happy that this produces truthful statements. You should be equally unhappy using such a form of question to the ouija board.

Questions To Ask

Very often, the most obvious approach is also the best. Simple questions tend to produce straightforward answers. You might try asking things like 'What was I in my last incarnation? When did I live? Where did I live? What was my name? What did I do? When did I die?'

At this stage it may have occurred to you that whether you are dealing with a spirit or with a product of your unconscious mind, you still stand a reasonable chance of getting a valid answer. If you are, in fact, speaking to a spirit suspended in some post-mortem limbo, or an elemental living in some weird alternative dimension, there remains the possibility that such an entity has access to the information you need. If, on the other hand, you favour the idea that you have tapped your own unconscious, then there is the possibility that you have also circumvented the birth/death trauma block.

Once you establish your ouija line of communication, you can expect direct and reasonable answers to the straightforward type of questions given in my example. But here the inherent weakness in ouija communication arises. Any attempt to establish further detail tends to be such a tedious affair that it is hardly worth the effort. Remember that each answer has to be spelled out letter by letter. Even a basic description of the previous environment could take several hours.

Disappointing though this may seem at first, you will find

that even sketchy information can form the basis of interesting developments. Indeed, nothing more than a name, date and place of birth is often enough to start you on a search for confirmation.

Begin with the place-name. If it is obscure, you may need to do a little detective work. The sound of the name should give you some indication of the country to which it belongs. Buy a detailed map and search it out. Once you have found your town, see if you can track down the name and date of birth. In Britain, parish registers are a mine of information. If the town is abroad, try writing for details to the municipal authorities. (Without, however, mentioning you are engaged in reincarnation research, otherwise you may not be taken seriously.)

The ouija makes a fascinating starting point in your exploration of past lives. But everything that has been said so far presupposes the ouija will work for you. This is by no means a certainty, at least where the standard ouija is concerned. It seems to require a certain type of personality (mediumistic, the spiritualists would say) and while most people have the faculty to some extent, many do not have it to the necessary degree. For them, the board remains inert.

There is, however, a different form of ouija which gets round this difficulty for almost everyone. And since it is a do-it-yourself affair, it has the added advantage of requiring no capital outlay.

All you need is a polished surface, an upturned glass, number and letter cards and the help of two or more friends. The polished surface is usually a table. If you do not have one to suit, try using a large mirror. Virtually any type of glass will do so long as it does not have a stem. Invert it, mouth downwards, on the middle of the table.

Here again, the letters of the alphabet and the numbers 0 to 9 are arranged in a circle as shown in the diagram, but

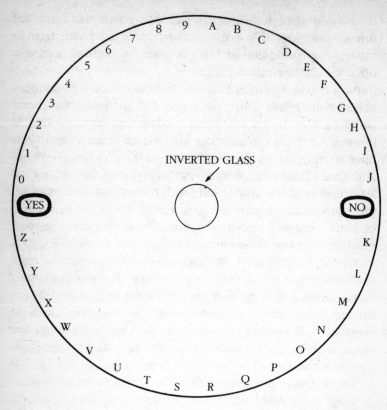

instead of using your whole hand as you would with the ouija board, place only the tip of a single finger lightly on the bottom of the glass, perferably at the rim. Your friends, seated round the table, should do the same.

The reason for company is that glass-moving, in my experience, cannot be done alone. The glass will move exactly as the ouija did, but it takes a minimum of three people to get it going. Four or five are better still, but if you go higher than six, the whole thing becomes unwieldy — there are only so many fingers you can fit on the bottom of a glass.

The problem with company is that you always run the risk of bringing in a joker. Some people find the urge to push the glass quite irresistible and the results perfectly hilarious. Unfortunately, there is no real way of detecting fraud when it is carried out with subtlety. Any answers you get from the glass will usually give the clue, of course, but you can waste a lot of time reaching that stage. Better to know your friends and debar anyone you feel will not co-operate fully.

Given a modicum of patience — you may have to sit for 10, 15, or perhaps even 20 minutes with your friends before the glass begins to move — you will find that this technique produces answers exactly as the ouija does, often with a great deal of speed and vigour. Results are often striking. A merchant seaman from Protestant Ulster discovers he was last time round ... a Jesuit. A puritanical young woman consults the board to find she was once the mistress of a nobleman. A British suburban housewife learns she sold flowers in the streets of Barcelona. A rally driver turns the clock back to find his last death was caused by an arrow in the back while running from Red Indians.

The stories, both in volume and variety, seem endless. A pleasant young civil servant was burned at the stake as a witch. A *femme fatale* now seems to be overcompensating for her last life as a nun. A writer, terrified of sailing, discovers he drowned when swept overboard during a life as a privateer.

All the above information originated from the same source. That is, the manifesting personality was identical in all cases. Two of the stories checked out reasonably well. The rest did not.

But to be fair, each of these reincarnatory histories *might* have been true. The problem with the majority was the lack of detail and lack of any written source of corroboration.

The entity which provided this information was, incidentally, impatient with sceptics. One plump Englishman, having learned he had been Henry VIII, felt this to be unlikely and returned to the board to ask, 'Have you changed your mind about what I was last time?'

'Y-E-S.

'Now who do you think I was?'

'Q-U-E-E-N O-F T-H-E F-A-I-R-I-E-S.'

CHAPTER EIGHT

HYPNOSIS

Hypnosis refers to a state or condition in which the subject becomes highly responsive to suggestions. The hypnotized individual seems to follow instructions in an uncritical, automatic fashion and attends closely only to those aspects of the environment made relevant by the hypnotist. If the subject is profoundly responsive, he or she hears, sees, feels, smells, and tastes in accordance with the suggestions given ...

Academic American Encyclopedia

Since Morey Bernstein wrote *The Search for Bridey Murphy,* hypnosis has attracted the attention of virtually everyone interested in a practical approach to reincarnation.

It has long been recognized that a subject under hypnosis could be regressed — brought back through suggestion to the days of his or her childhood. That this regression was genuine was shown time and again when infantile characteristics appeared. Childhood peculiarities which the subject had forgotten — at least consciously — suddenly reappeared.

One of the most striking examples of this phenomenon involves handedness. For many years, the educational system of our predominantly right-handed culture made a point of persuading left-handed children to switch to using their right hands. Once this was achieved, typically at an early age and all too often as the result of corporal punishment, the child quickly forgot left-handed skills, and eventually would forget ever having been left-handed at all. When hypnotically regressed as an adult, however, those same left-handed skills will instantly return once the subject is taken back beyond the point of change.

Not only can lost skills be recovered, but learned skills can be forgotten in the process of regression. The definitive experiment which established this fact proved embarrassing both to the subject and the psychiatrist who placed him in trance. The man regressed with ease to babyhood, then promptly voided urine in his trousers. He had passed back beyond the age when bladder control was established. Experiments like these, along with careful questioning of (older) relatives and friends, quickly established that regressed subjects were indeed able to produce accurate memories which were lost to them in their normal waking state.

As mentioned earlier, several of the less orthodox Freudian psychiatrists have claimed that hypnosis (and even in some cases depth analysis) will produce memories from the womb itself.

Beyond the Womb

But Morey Bernstein was one of a number of experimenters who went further. Working with a Colorado housewife named Virginia Tighe (whom he was to call 'Ruth Simmons' in his published account), he managed to generate a regression which went beyond the point of conception and unearthed information about a previous existence in Belfast, Northern Ireland, as Bridey Murphy. As the sessions continued, it transpired that Bridey Murphy was born in County Cork in 1798. The experiments provided considerable detail about Ireland in the nineteenth century. Mrs Tighe talked about coinage, food, furniture, books, popular songs, farming methods and much more. She was able to give the names of shops and frequently used obscure and obsolete words, such as 'flats' (meaning platters).

Much of the information checked out. The entranced Virginia Tighe actually confounded experts, who were convinced iron bedsteads had not been used in Ireland prior to 1850. As Bridey, she claimed to have slept in one. Subsequent investigation showed such bedsteads advertised as early as 1802.

A number of the sessions were recorded and broadcast. Both the book outlining the experiments (*The Search for Bridey Murphy,* which became an international best-seller in the early 1950s) and the recordings sparked off a long-running controversy. Experts, who tend to be self-appointed in these cases, pronounced for and against the validity of the Bernstein experiment. It was eventually discovered that Mrs Tighe had had an Irish nurse in her own childhood, and the assumption was made that much of the information had really been drawn from her. This did not explain how the nurse was supposed to know about things like iron bedsteads when the historians did not. If there was an overall result for the proverbial person in the street, it must have been sheer confusion.

Bernstein's flair for promotion eclipsed the fact that a

great many others have tried a similar approach with similar results. In Wales, for example, Arnall and Dulcie Bloxham conducted hypnotic investigations into reincarnation, producing, over a period of years, many hundreds of hours of tape recordings. In the north of England, the investigator Joe Keeton has done essentially the same thing and frequently demonstrated reincarnatory regression in public. In my own small way, I have managed a number of similar experiments myself.

But can experiments of this type really produce valid memories of past lives? The direct answer is yes ... with reservations. This excerpt from an article in the *New Grolier Electronic Encyclopedia* puts is succinctly:

> ... although age regression is useful in psychotherapeutic treatment, the memories called forth may validly reflect the individual's feelings about past events; the events that are relived, however, may or may not be historically accurate. Although compelling, both to the subject and to the observer, these memories often are in fact a combination of many events, not only from the same epoch but also confounded by later experiences — a matter of concern if historical accuracy is important, as in legal matters.

The quote, in context, refers to regression within the current lifeline, but its observations are equally valid when applied to past-life research. Like the ouija information, every item obtained from the unconscious during trance must be checked and rechecked before it is accepted.

Before embarking on your own experiments in this field, it is as well to realize what you are getting into.

No Toy

Hypnosis is not a toy. While properly handled it has few inherent dangers, proper handling is important. When you induce trance in a subject, you form a very definite relationship with him or her. And this relationship has serious responsibilities. The human mind is a delicate instrument. To probe its depths without consideration of this fact is asking for trouble.

In reincarnation research, strong emotions are often stirred. Under depth hypnosis, these emotions are not simply remembered, but subjectively relived. In some cases, the subject cannot discriminate between the regression experience and literal physical reality. Unless the operator takes great care, a sort of psychic storm can easily blow up with most unpleasant results. Treat your subjects gently and with sympathy. If your questions produce reluctance, do not try to batter down the block. Switch to another tack. Also make a careful note of any results. Memory, in cases of emotional drama, is notoriously unreliable.

How to Induce Hypnosis

Since the theory of animal magnetism was abandoned,* the cause of hypnosis has remained largely an open question. We know that what typically occurs is that the subject is asked to relax and focus his or her attention, usually on

---

* Abandoned, that is, as an explanation of hypnosis. There is increasing evidence, notably from Eastern Europe, that a force very like the old 'animal magnetism' may actually exist.

some object. It is suggested, in a quiet, compelling tone, that relaxation will increase and the eyes grow tired. Soon the eyelids begin to flutter, at which time it is suggested they close. The subject's eyes do shut, and he or she begins to show signs of profound relaxation, with quiet, regular breathing, superficially resembling sleep. It may now be suggested that the subject's eyes are so heavy that he or she cannot open them. When invited to try, the subject finds often with surprise, that the eyes will not open.

Suggestion certainly plays a part in this process, but most of the real work seems to be done by the subject. Some people seem to drop into trance at the wave of a hand. (A friend of mine once slid off the chair while I was engaged in hypnotizing someone else.) Others defy all the rules. One of London's best-known psychologists, Professor H.J. Eysenck, quotes the case of a subject who failed to achieve even light trance after some hundreds of hours of patient work by a skilled medical hypnotist.

Eventually the doctor lost his temper and roared, 'For —'s sake go to sleep, you silly —!'

At which the patient immediately passed into trance.

The anecdote illustrates the fact that there are several ways to induce hypnosis. But unless you have previous experience, you best approach is to search for a subject who reacts well, then follow orthodox procedure.

Whatever small variation on the basic methods you decide to use, you will almost always begin by encouraging the subject to relax.

Conscious Relaxation

In these troubled times, very few people find relaxation easy. Consequently, the best approach is to do it consciously. Begin by making it easy for the subject. Let him or her sit in a comfortable chair, or stretch out on a couch or bed. Make sure the room is quiet, with as few distractions as possible. It is a good idea to dim the lights, although total darkness should be avoided. Try to ensure there will be no interruptions. If necessary, turn the key in the lock. If there is a phone in the room, take it off the hook.

Explain to your subject that until he or she recognizes tension there is little chance of achieving relaxation. Consequently he or she must contract each set of muscles in sequence, feeling the tension, then letting go. Actually take him or her through the sequence, starting at the feet and working upwards through the muscle groupings of the body. You can use the following sequence as a guide to the sort of thing you should be saying:

Concentrate on your feet. Wiggle them about. Curl them to tense the muscles, think about the tension, experience how it feels, then allow them to relax. Now think about the sensation of relaxation, noting how it differs from the tension.

Concentrate next on your calf muscles. Tighten and relax them, thinking about the tension and the relaxation in the same way as before.

Concentrate on your thigh muscles. Tighten and relax them, again thinking about the tension and the relaxation. Now continue in the following sequence, in each case pausing to think about the feelings generated both by tension and relaxation:

Concentrate on your buttock muscles. Tighten your buttocks and anus, then relax them.

Concentrate on your stomach muscles, a very common tension focus. Tighten, then relax them.

Concentrate on your hands. Curl them into fists, then relax them.

Concentrate on your arms. Tighten them rigidly, then relax them.

Concentrate on your back. Tighten the muscles, then relax them.

Concentrate on your chest. Tighten the muscles, then relax them.

Concentrate on your shoulders, another very common tension focus. Hunch your shoulders to tighten the muscles, then relax them.

Concentrate on your neck. Tighten the muscles, then relax them.

Concentrate on your face. Grit your teeth and contort your features to tense up the facial muscles, then relax them.

Concentrate on your scalp. Frown to tighten the scalp muscles, then relax them.

Now tighten up every muscle in your body, holding your entire body momentarily rigid, then relax, letting go as completely as you are able. Do this final whole body sequence again, then again — three times in all. On the third time, take a really deep breath when you tense the muscles and sigh deeply aloud as you let the tension go.

Properly carried out, this exercise produces a considerable degree of relaxation.

Ask your subject to breathe deeply. This increases the supply of oxygen to the bloodstream and hence to the brain and muscles, helping towards a further degree of relaxation.

In hypnosis, there is no battle of wills, despite popular imaginings. Where such a battle occurs, the subject will win and hypnosis is not possible. Make sure your subject knows this. To induce trance, you will need every ounce of co-operation, especially in the early stages.

Suggestion Sequences

Once your subject is totally relaxed, begin a sequence of suggestion. The technique you are going to use involves 'stacking' increasingly complex suggestions until a satisfactory trance level is achieved. It is based on the theory that a subject persuaded to accept one suggestion is more likely to accept another; and that the second suggestion may be structured to push things a little further than the first. The subject is slowly led further and further from normal consciousness, one small step at a time.

Begin the process by asking your subject to open his (or her) eyes (if they are closed) and gaze at a spot above eye level. You can, if you wish, hold something for the subject to look at, but a crack in the ceiling or a picture on the wall will do just as well. The important thing is that the subject is forced to look upwards. This causes the eyes to tire quite quickly. Begin the hypnotic induction by telling him quietly, firmly and repeatedly that his eyes are growing tired. Your subject will accept the initial suggestion because it happens to be true: his eyes really *are* getting tired. Then, having accepted your first suggestion, it is all the more likely that your second will also be accepted.

Your second suggestion builds on the first. You should suggest quietly, firmly and repeatedly, that your subject's eyelids are growing heavy.

Like your first suggestion, this one is something of a cheat. Once your eyes begin to tire, your body will start to issue increasingly urgent demands that you rest them. But your subject is being made to maintain the position which produced the tiredness, still looking upwards, eyes fully open, vision focused on a specific point, unable to ease the tiredness by looking at something else. Thus his body will seek to persuade him to close his eyes. But he cannot do this either (because you have instructed him to keep his eyes open.) A conflict arises. His eyelids will begin to droop, then snap open. Your first indication of success in your technique will be the flickering of the eyelids which arises out of this conflict.

Throughout, you are, of course, continuing to insist that your subject's eyelids are growing heavy — which is, of course, exactly what he is feeling. Another suggestion has been accepted and your subject is consequently more predisposed to accept the next. Once you have spotted the distinctive flicker, suggest that his eyelids are now so heavy they can no longer stay open. This suggestion is often accepted very quickly, and the eyelids close.

Continue to deliver suggestions in a low, firm, confident tone. When an easy rhythm is established, begin to suggest that your subject is experiencing the sensation of total relaxation. You have increased the acceptability of this suggestion by talking through the physical relaxation process. He should certainly be nicely relaxed by now, so once again your suggestions are building on a physical reality. To the relaxation suggestion add the further suggestion that he feels incapable of activity — a state which tends to follow relaxation naturally, thus guaranteeing the acceptance of yet another suggestion.

At this stage, your suggestions should be aimed towards increasing the degree of relaxation. ('Your body is becoming heavy. You are feeling more and more relaxed.') Later, you can switch to suggestions that your subject is becoming sleepy, is falling asleep, is falling deeper asleep.

It is as well to note here that a subject under hypnosis does not actually fall asleep. Indeed, if he did, you would lose your influence over him altogether. But in your sequence of suggestions, you are speaking primarily to the subject's unconscious mind and must do so in the language it understands. Total relaxation, which is the strongest indication of the trance state, is associated by the unconscious with sleep — hence the suggestion.

Try to inject a certain amount of colour and imagery into your suggestions, as again this helps them take root.

At this stage, suggest a number of times that your subject will find it impossible to raise his arm. Then invite him to try. If everything is going according to schedule, the arm should remain firmly where it was. Move on to the suggestion that your subject is drifting and feels miles away. Add to this the suggestion that he feels a pleasant, relaxing warmth throughout his body.

Have patience. The time taken for hypnotic induction varies from subject to subject. Some go under remarkably quickly, but it is best to assume you will have to invest a considerable amount of effort. Repeat suggestions over and over, reinforcing their effect. Pay close attention to your subject, who will often give clear indications of how comfortable or otherwise he is with the induction process.

Trance Levels

There are several levels of hypnotic trance. As you gain experience, you will certainly discover subjects whose trances fall into the following categories:

Insusceptible. Here subjects show a total lack of response to suggestion. The technique simply does not work at any level.

Hypnoidal. The characteristics of this state are relaxation, some fluttering of the eyelids usually followed by actual closing of the eyes. Subjectively the body feels heavy.

Light Trance. When this level is achieved, it becomes virtually impossible for subjects to open their eyes or move their limbs without specific instructions. Suggestions of rigidity are readily accepted and it is possible to induce what is technically termed 'glove anaesthesia', where no pain can be felt in the hands (in the area covered by a glove).

Medium Trance. Here spontaneous amnesia arises — a partial or total inability to remember what happened during trance. Subjects may be persuaded to undergo temporary personality changes, and will react to simple post-hypnotic suggestions, including post-hypnotic anaesthesia.

Deep Trance. Deep trance is characterized by your subjects' ability to open their eyes without affecting the trance, the acceptance of bizarre and complex post-hypnotic suggestions, including post-hypnotic hallucination, auditory hallucinations and selective directed post-hypnotic amnesia.

Although it is possible (if only just and only sometimes) to explore memories of past incarnations under light trance, a minimum of medium trance is recommended for serious work.

Regressing the Subject

Once you have your subject in trance, regression is a simple enough affair. But take your time and do it gradually.

Start by suggesting that your subject is going back in time to his last birthday. Tell him he can remember vividly what he did and where he went. Then suggest he is travelling further back in time ... five years now, then ten. Suggest 'stops' along the way and encourage him to tell you what he sees.

Make certain to suggest as strongly as you can that no matter how far he travels back or where he seems to find himself, he will always hear your voice and obey your instructions.

In this way, bring him right back to childhood, then babyhood. You will almost certainly notice strong reactions at this stage. Thumb-sucking may manifest, or crying. It is especially important here to suggest he is safe and well and that no harm can befall him.

When your subject has regressed to early childhood, you are ready to take him on the major journey beyond birth into his last incarnation. Remember your subject's sensitivities and avoid the areas of birth and death trauma. Do *not* suggest he is sinking back into the womb, or he may go into a state of withdrawal. Instead, simply tell him he is making a major leap in time, far back beyond the moment of his birth. Then ask him what he is experiencing. And take careful note of what he says.

Limbo State

Not everyone lands directly into a previous existence. A number of subjects, including Virginia Tighe, report a curious limbo state in some different plane or dimension. This state has considerable interest in itself, but since it is reincarnatory information you want, you must take your subject gently beyond it to his last life.

Avoid questions which may upset him, but do press for detail. A woolly vision of a landscape, coupled with a hazy idea of time, is worse than useless. You need dates, names and places if you are going to investigate properly. Probe for these things gently, but miss no opportunity to discover them.

Bringing your subject out of trance is quite straightforward. Tell him that you are going to count to three. Suggest that on the final count he will open his eyes and that as he does so, he will instantly become alert and fully aware of everything that is going on around him. Tell him that he will feel relaxed, happy and invigorated, as if he had just emerged from a deep, refreshing sleep, and that he will remember clearly, in detail, everything he has experienced. (Avoid negative suggestions, such as 'You will have no headache.' The mind has an unhappy knack of missing that little word *no* and providing just the condition you wish to avoid.) Having given these suggestions a few times, count firmly to three and encourage the subject to waken.

Almost every subject will come out of trance on cue. For the few who are tardy, simply repeat the process. Very rarely indeed will you be required to repeat it more than once.

Self-Hypnosis

Exploring someone else's past lives is interesting, but not half so interesting as exploring your own. If you decide the techniques of hypnosis will give you the best chance to do so, then your next step must be to learn something about self-hypnosis.

There are two ways of inducing self-hypnosis, one easy, one hard. The easy way is to have a skilled hypnotist put you into trance and give you a special keyword which you can use to do the job yourself in future.

The suggestion might go something like this: 'You are now deeply asleep. In a moment I am going to waken you. But before I do, I want you to know that each time you repeat the word "*dreamsleep*" aloud, you will immediately fall as deeply asleep as you are sleeping now. The word is "*dreamsleep*". Should another person pronounce it, it will have no effect on you. But once *you* pronounce it aloud, you will fall as deeply asleep as you are sleeping now. But though asleep, you will retain control. You will be able to direct your mind wherever you wish it to go. You will be able to control your body and emotions while you are in this deep sleep.'

It is as well to select a composite or nonsense word as your key. There is nothing more embarrassing than sending yourself into trance with a chance remark to a friend.

When you wish to start your explorations of your past lives, it then becomes a matter of relaxing in suitable circumstances, repeating your key word and taking off.

The hard way to induce self-hypnosis is to go it alone. Oddly enough, the technique is almost identical to that used in putting a subject into trance. The only real difference is that the subject is yourself.

Arrange for a quiet, semi-darkened room, sit or lie down and go through the conscious relaxation process. When you are fully relaxed, give yourself (mentally) the relevant suggestions. Unless you are very lucky, you will not achieve success right away. But if you keep at it, the level of trance will gradually deepen.

Once you are satisfied with the trance level, proceed with the regression process — again in exactly the same way as if you were working with a subject. Take yourself slowly back over the years, then make the leap that will bring you beyond the point of your last birth.

Drawback

The major drawback with both hypnosis and self-hypnosis as an aid to reincarnatory exploration is that at least a medium trance level must be achieved before there is any likelihood of success. According to Professor H.J. Eysenck, only about 25 per cent of the population are capable of reaching medium trance level, and even fewer (about 20 per cent) will sink into deep trance. My own experience suggests that the figure for medium trance might be higher, but deep trance subjects are certainly rare.

However the figures break down, there is no getting around the problem. Unless you can achieve a reasonable level of trance, hypnosis will not provide you with a key to past lives. Fortunately, hypnosis is not the only key, although in cases where it does work, it tends to be by far the easiest, most accurate and most spectacular.

CHAPTER NINE

ARCHETYPAL CONTEMPLATION

Archetype: A term derived from the psychological theories of Carl Jung, who posited the existence of a 'collective unconscious' containing images that are recognized by all people. An archetype is therefore a symbol whose significance is universal.

Academic American Encyclopedia

Many occult techniques stand unsupported by reasonable theory. Their followers apply them on a purely empirical basis without having the slightest idea why results follow. But archetypal contemplation is an exception to this rule. The practice, in fact, grew directly out of theory.

Let us look first at the theory. Very few believers in reincarnation ever stop to ask themselves a very basic question, namely, exactly *what* reincarnates? We have already touched on this problem when we discussed the theory of an Oversoul (see Chapter 6), but the time has now come to examine this subject in a little more detail.

You exist. You have always existed. You will always exist. There is no way you can avoid this. It is as much a fact (and more) as the book in your hands. What does 'you' mean in this context? Certainly not the body you happen to be wearing now. Like it or not, that body will disintegrate at some time. Nor are 'you' your personality. Think about it for a moment before you are tempted to disagree. Your personality at seven months was very different to the personality you have today. Your personality in 20 years time will be different again.

If this aspect of your psyche cannot even survive physical existence, what chance has it of surviving eternity? The occultist postulates something far beyond personality or even thought. He teaches the existence of an inner 'you', unchanging and eternal, a spark of the divine, almost beyond understanding. It is this 'you' which exists in the ultimate sense.

Occult Exercise

There is a curious occult exercise which you might try (although not too often, as it tends to be disturbing). Imagine yourself without your body, a disembodied mind. Then imagine yourself without your imagination, floating in a dark and silent realm of abstract thoughts. Now imagine yourself without your thoughts. Nothing is left ... and yet, incredibly, you continue to exist.

This little exercise will bring you as close as you can get to the innermost, eternal 'you'.

Take the exercise a step further. Forget you ever had a body, personality or mind. Imagine yourself simply existing and nothing more. Now assume it is part of your nature to gain experience. This is not a question of desire, or will. Call it, if anything, a reaction to evolutionary pressure. There is no way for you to gain experience in your current state, so, as a reaction to evolutionary pressure, you build up a mind and personality and attach them to a body. In short, you incarnate.

After a number of years (and heaven knows what the determining factor is here) you withdraw the mind and personality from the body you've been using and absorb the experience into your own being. From the physical point of view, you have died. This sending forth and subsequent withdrawal becomes a standard pattern. Each time it happens, you reincarnate.

Eventually you reach a stage where you have experienced enough. Certain signs appear once this point is reached. Orientals recognize them as the signs of Buddhahood. You no longer need to reincarnate. In a changed form, you continue to exist. If — and this is high metaphysical speculation — it is necessary for you to evolve further, it must be in some other direction.

Jungian Concepts

In the Jungian school of psychology, there are two commonly-used terms which seem related to the notion of the inner 'you' we have been discussing. One is Self. The other is Collective Unconscious.

The Self, to greatly simplify Jung's concept, is the central point of the psyche, the mind's ultimate fulcrum of stability. Once the little old familiar 'you' (the Ego) achieves integration with the Self, you have unified your entire psychic structure.

The Collective Unconscious is a level of the mind common to humanity as a whole, the group mind of the race, the psychic expression of humanity's collective experience over millennia. Jung refers to it as a brooding giant, dreaming ancient dreams.

Even if you leave the Self aside for a moment (although the Self and the Collective Unconscious should properly be considered together), it is not difficult to equate the Collective Unconscious with the innermost 'you'. I would suggest the two coincide completely, but for practical purposes you can allow yourself this leeway without affecting the outcome.

Let's come back down to earth now. Your immediate problem is that of investigating past incarnations.

If you accept the theory I have just outlined, then the storehouse of experiences from your past lives is the area of Collective Unconscious in the depths of your psyche. How then do you reach this area?

Potent Forces

The first question you must ask yourself is, do you really want to? Powerful forces play in the Collective Unconscious. Do you really want to disturb them? The question may seem faintly superstitious, bordering on medieval warnings about dealings with the devil, but it is intended seriously enough. If you are prepared to take your chances, then investigate the archetypes.

According to Jung, an archetype is a foundation stone of the mind. This tells us everything ... and nothing. The idea of an archetype is not easy to grasp. Often paradox is involved. Jung himself, for instance, had no difficulty in reconciling the ideas of God as an archetype and God as a cosmic reality.

Typically, you must personalize the archetypes before you confront them. On doing so, you will find them personalities of great power. Quite often, this power has an obsessive quality, which is one of the major dangers of monkeying with the archetypes in the first place. Even without conscious effort, hundreds of thousands of men and women have condemned themselves to an archetypal existence, obsessed by a pattern of behaviour, submerging their personalities to the forces that well up from the deep unconscious.

Archetypal Symbols

There are many, many archetypal symbols. A short list of the main ones follows: The Father; The Mother; The King; The Fool; The Old Wise Woman; The Hermit; The Slave; The Messenger; The Warrior; The Enchantress; The Magician.

These symbols are, of course, personalized. Among others, more abstract in nature, are: The Circle; The Cross; The Swastika (dangerous to use now, in view of its Nazi overlay); The Sun; The Point; The Yin and the Yang.

Numbers — at least those from one to nine — are often held to be archetypal.

I would suggest choosing one of the abstract symbols for your experiments. Any results tend to be slower and less spectacular than with the personalized ones, but infinitely safer. Use the symbol regularly, don't expect too much even in the long run, and expect absolutely nothing on your first few attempts.

Contemplation of a symbol can be damnably difficult until you get the hang of it. But what you do is easy enough to outline. Begin by visualizing your chosen symbol. You may, if you wish, first draw it on a piece of paper. When you are visualizing clearly, hold it.

That's all there is to it. You simply contemplate the symbol quietly and calmly, ignoring all extraneous thoughts. You are not even thinking *about* the symbol, merely allowing it to fill your mind.

Energy Channel

Used in this way, an archetypal symbol eventually becomes a channel for energies arising in the deep unconscious. Your original desire to explore past lives forms, so to speak, a framework for these forces (and for that reason should never be forgotten).

It is as if your mind becomes sensitized by the symbol. You will find, as time and regular daily practice of contemplation goes on, that flashes of unfamiliar scenes begin to pass before your inner eye. Take a note of these fragments, for they are clues to prior lives.

This technique, perhaps more than most, is uncertain and requires the most rigorous checking out. But for those who find they can make use of it, it will sometimes produce results where all other approaches fail. Short of archetypal obsession, which is fairly easily avoided if you confine yourself to use of abstract symbols, the only real danger is losing control of your visions. To find inner pictures arising erratically is a nuisance at best, so it is worthwhile adopting the old occult procedure of a ritual gesture before and after contemplation. The gesture (the Sign of the Cross, for instance) clearly marks the outer limits of your experiments and prevents any trouble later.

One final word. The visions are inward ones. Should they at any point become objective, abandon your experiments at once and see a good psychiatrist.

CHAPTER TEN

DEPTH MEDITATION

Meditation is the method of realizing, or reflectively
considering, a religious truth in order to arrive at a
personal understanding and love for what it signifies.
It is an important part of Buddhism and Hinduism but
also appears in Christianity and Islam. Although
usually considered a means toward developing the
spiritual life of a religious person, meditation is not
necessarily a religious practice.

Academic American Encyclopedia

In the East, the royal road to wisdom is meditation. Based,
as it is, on the assumption that all real knowledge must
ultimately come from within, the technique is held in such
awe that certain of the ancient Hindu sources maintain its
practice will actually produce magical powers like
invisibility or the ability to levitate.

The amount of awe meditation engenders in the West is
only slightly less, although the basic superstitions differ

greatly. Here the greatest superstition surrounding meditation is that it is something mysterious and difficult to learn. I once met a young woman who had studied books on yoga for more than five years in the hope that, eventually, she might 'evolve enough to attempt to meditate'.

The strange thing is that numerous Westerners have practised forms of meditation all their lives but, like the man who wrote prose, might be surprised to learn it. At its most simple, meditation on a subject means no more than brooding over it. Once you realize that, you realize that you have meditated frequently in the past. You have taken your worries and brooded over them, turning them in your mind to examine each and every angle. And at times, this examination has produced sudden results. A new approach has struck you, a fresh solution. In the language of the Orient, you achieved, through meditation, an illumination.

Difference of Degree

You may be tempted to protest that this type of mundane brooding can scarcely be the same powerful technique as used by saints, yogis and gurus. Yet the difference is purely one of degree. Where the yogi or the saint scores over the average person, is that the former meditates *regularly*. While this is, as you can see, a difference of degree, it is a difference which produces such striking results that it might as well be a difference of essence.

A parallel may make the point clear. In karate, the deadly Oriental form of unarmed combat, adepts toughen up their hands by punching a sackful of sand. There is no secret in the technique (at least not any more). Indeed you may even have punched a sackful of sand yourself at some time in your life. The difference between your hands and those of a karate adept is that his can split a brick in half or punch through an inch-thick board. And this difference was achieved by nothing more than regularity of practice.

In the mental realm, the yoga adept will meditate each day for hours on end. Some go further and set aside whole weeks, months, or even years for continuous meditation. The result of this continuous activity is rather like the result of water dripping on a stone — something wears away. In the case of the yogi, what wears away is the psychic barrier between conscious and unconscious levels of the mind. A channel is, so to speak, bored through, a well is sunk, and out of this shaft flows the knowledge and wisdom of the unconscious.

Once you find a method that allows you to reach your own unconscious, you have found a method that promises — at least potentially — to deliver information about your last incarnation.

Several Forms

There are, as it happens, several forms of meditation, with a multitude of aids to the ultimate result. Some schools, such as that of the Maharishi, advocate the use of a mantram. One Chinese group I came across advocated the adoption of the lotus posture with the eyes fixed on the tip of the nose. Unfortunately the lotus posture is a physical impossibility for most Westerners, and staring at the tip of the nose tends to produce headache rather than enlightenment.

But these are embellishments, useful in some cases, but

unnecessary if you are prepared to use a little patience and perseverance. Two genuine prerequisites to effective meditation are relaxation and concentration. But do not worry too much if you are tense and woolly-minded: both relaxation and concentration can be developed, just as Mr Universe may be developed from the proverbial seven-stone weakling.

Begin your meditation routine by choosing your time, your place and your chair. If meditation is to be worth anything at all to you — and certainly if you intend to use it as a technique for the exploration of previous lives — it must be practised regularly. And that means setting aside a specific time each day.

There is no need to overdo it. In fact extremism is as much to be avoided here as in other walks of life. Yogis may spend several years in meditation. You would be well advised to begin with several minutes. Even when you get the hang of the system, an hour a day is about the optimum for the average Westerner. Perhaps the most workable period is half that time — but work up to it gradually.

In the East, morning is the traditional meditation time. Unlike so many Eastern traditions, this one transplants perfectly into the West. If you meditate in the morning, your mind will be fresh and alert; and because the world is lazy, there will be far less chance of disturbance.

Having picked your time, now choose your place. It should be quiet, warm and free from disturbance. Anyone who meditates in a room with a phone is asking for trouble. The quiet, warm, disturbance-free room may be a counsel of perfection, but try to come as close to it as possible. The yogi — and even you yourself at a later stage — may be able to ignore outside noise. But in the beginning you will not.

Tumo adepts may dry soaking blankets with their body

heat, but unless you can find a Tibetan to teach you this discipline, you will be a victim of temperature. No one meditates successfully while wondering when his frost-bitten toes will require amputation.

Choice of Chair

Having decided on your time and picked the best possible place, choose your chair. As the careful cultivation of the lotus pose is vital to the yogi, so the careful choice of a chair is vital to the Occidental practitioner of meditation. And for essentially the same reason. The contortions needed to achieve the lotus pose are only painful to those of us whose limbs have been conditioned to a Western environment. Given an Oriental background and a few years' practice, the lotus posture is one of the most comfortable known to man. The placing of the limbs produces a sort of anaesthesia below the waist with the result that those common little aches and pains the flesh is heir to disappear at once.

Despite their strange ways, yogis have a considerable store of common sense. They argue that meditation is easier without distractions, and further, that most distractions come from the body. So an important part of any meditation technique must be to keep the body happy, hence the anaesthetic lotus posture. You can take the benefit of this logic without necessarily adopting yogic postures. A comfortable chair will usually keep a Western body happy. But there is a danger here. If the chair you pick is *too* comfortable, you run a considerable risk of falling asleep. And no one can meditate while unconscious. The happy medium seems to be a comfortable upright chair. Your body is happy, but the possibility of falling off will keep you awake.

Learning to Meditate

So far, the considerations have been largely physical, and relatively easy. The next considerations are largely psychological and consequently difficult, or at least time-consuming.

Perhaps the greatest drawback to the use of meditation as a key to your past lives is that you have first to learn to meditate, then, having learned, you must learn to use the technique in a very special way. The sequence is time-consuming, but well worth while. Even should you never learn you once were Julius Caesar, meditation is worth practising for its own sake. While it may not help you to levitate, it can work greater magic, such as the development of a peaceful mind and the production of a fuller life.

The only way to learn to meditate is to do it. There must be hundreds of books promising to teach you meditation's secrets. But all the information comes back to one thing in the end: you must take action in order to learn.

Begin at your appointed time tomorrow. Sit down in your chosen chair in your chosen room. And relax. My few brief remarks about relaxation during the earlier section on hypnosis are relevant here. Most people have lost the knack. (They had it once, as you'll notice if you ever watch a baby sleeping.) And having lost the knack, they must be taught — or teach themselves — to relax.

So go through a conscious relaxation process. Start with your feet. Curl the toes, tensing the muscles until they hurt, then let go. And do this with each set of muscles all along your body. You'll soon get the hang of it; and when you do, you'll find the totally relaxed state a lot more pleasant than the latent tension that grips most of us.

When you have achieved relaxation, get to grips with your subject. *But the subject, at this stage, should not be your past lives.* You are learning to meditate. Until you have learnt, you cannot use meditation as a tool for reincarnatory research.

This may jar a little in the light of my earlier remarks that meditation, per se, is simple and that many have been meditating unconsciously for most of their lives. But to recall an earlier analogy, the fact that you write prose each time you pen a letter to a friend does not mean you are the equal of Shaw or Wilde or Dickens or, indeed, John Creasey.

A good idea is to pick an interesting book, preferably of a philosophical or mystical nature (although the technique works equally well with scientific volumes), read a chapter, then meditate on the content. This approach has the added advantage of providing a bulk of ideas to hold your attention.

Meditation Technique

In meditation, you simply think about the subject of your choice, following up each train of thought as it arises. But you think about the subject exclusively, rejecting all notions which arise from other sources.

This is the difficult bit, and the bit that only comes with practice. At first you will find your mind wandering time and time again. You will wonder if you will ever get it under control. But practice helps. And though the heights of yogic concentration may never be yours, they are not necessary for your purpose. After a few weeks or months, you will find that your concentration is greatly improved and that relaxation has become something of a habit. At that stage, you are on the brink of genuine meditation.

The testing factor in meditation is the emergence of fresh light. If new ideas emerge, if old puzzles are suddenly solved, you may rest assured that you are meditating properly, that you are beginning to sink the well into your own unconscious. Don't hurry and don't force it. There is plenty of time. Make sure you are absolutely familiar with the meditation technique before putting it to use for reincarnation research.

Meditation and Past Lives

When using meditation to obtain information on your past lives, it is necessary to use an oblique approach. It is pointless meditating on the problem of what you were last time round because of the embarrassing richness of possibilities your mind will throw up. Soldier, sailor, tinker, tailor, rich man, poor man, beggerman, thief ... and a thousand more will turn up on parade, all claiming your attention, all hoping for your allegiance.

Instead, meditate on the mechanics of reincarnation itself. Begin by soaking up as much information as you can from published sources. Examine Buddhist, Hindu and Theosophical thought on the subject. Follow up some of the less orthodox approaches, such as Ouspensky's ideas on Eternal Recurrence. Try to relate what you learn to what you know of psychology, both occult and orthodox.

As you continue a series of meditations on reincarnation,

an odd thing happens. Your unconscious, in producing illustration for the particular theory of reincarnation it wishes to teach you, will draw on (or at least tend to draw on) examples from your own past life. As usual, these examples must be carefully checked out before they are accepted. And it is as well to appreciate that the theory of reincarnation your unconscious has formulated may not be correct either. Even in occult pursuits, nothing takes the place of scientific corroboration.

CHAPTER ELEVEN

THE AKASHIC RECORD

A library is an organized collection of books and other
informational materials covering the whole field of
knowledge or any part of it; a library may be available
to everyone or restricted to a particular community ...
The organization of its contents is the main
characteristic distinguishing a library from a collection
of books — that is, the orderly arrangement of
materials by some form of classification and their
record and description by means of a card catalogue.

Academic American Encyclopedia

When Edgar Cayce, the most remarkable clairvoyant
America had ever produced, wanted to discover
information about somebody's past lives, he went to a
familiar library and picked out the relevant book. But the
library was familiar only to Cayce. For it did not exist on the
physical plane.

During the time Edgar Cayce was awake, he proved to

be a highly religious, poorly educated, not very interesting photographer. Only under hypnosis did he become an astonishingly successful healer, an extraordinary prophet and — no single word exists for it — an investigator into past incarnations.

Consequently, Cayce's library trips were (from one point of view) hallucinations. But they were hallucinations which produced amazingly accurate information, so that they can hardly be viewed in the same light as the alcoholic's pink elephants or the monsters in the corners of a schizophrenic mind.

Leaving aside the form of his vision, it is obvious that Cayce, at a certain level of consciousness, was able to tap something that had the earmarks of a universal source of information.

Ancient Tradition

Cayce was not, except by accident, an occultist. In waking life, his beliefs were fundamental, only slowly modified by the information filtered through his unconscious. Had he been an occultist, he would certainly have been familiar with the ancient tradition of an Akashic Record.

Coherent information on the Akashic Record is difficult to come by. It seems, in essence, to be an Eastern version of the Book of Life. But instead of being a supernatural scribe, as the medieval Westerner believed, the record of all things, events, actions and beliefs is somehow preserved in the very fabric of the universe itself.

One prolific occult writer has pointed to modern findings to show this notion may not be quite as fanciful as it sounds. We may, for instance, use a telescope to watch events which took place many thousands of years ago. Light moves at a crawl in interstellar space, so that we see the stars not as they are, but as they were.

It is a small enough switch to imagine ourselves distant from Earth, examining its light rays. Assuming a powerful enough telescope, it would, in theory, be possible to watch the Battle of Hastings or the death of Christ. (In practice, regrettably, a telescope to do the trick simply could not be built, even assuming all the other conditions were met.)

Despite this interesting analogy, the Akashic Record seems to have very little to do with light. It may, however, have something to do with that curious occult background element, ether. Yogis and charlatans have claimed the ability to read the Akashic, but neither class appears overly anxious to describe what happens when they do. The few descriptions which have crept into literature (such as Cayce's library) are usually quite contradictory in form.

Astral Plane

To the layman, contradiction points to fraud or nonsense. To the occultist, it will frequently suggest the Astral Plane.

This is not, primarily, a book for the skilled occultist, so that until now I have avoided the technical terms of occultism as much as possible. Since I see no further possibility of avoiding one of the most difficult, for this section at least, I propose to take a moment to define and explain it as clearly as possible.

The Astral Plan (or Astral Light) is an omnipresent, non-physical, plastic, fluid medium which, while formless in itself, has the property of taking on or reflecting any form impressed upon it.

So much for the definition which, while comprehensive, is not particularly easy to follow. Fortunately, the Astral Plane does not have to be grasped intellectually since the vast majority of people have a psychological faculty which enables them to sense it directly. This faculty is imagination. When you make a picture in your mind, you are operating on the Astral Plane. This is not to say that the Astral Plane is simply another term for your imagination. It is to say that when you use your imagination, you work on the basic 'material' of the Astral Plane.

There are degrees of imagination and consequently there are degrees of contact with the Astral. In so far as image-building is concerned, a daydream follows the same basic mechanics as a sleeping dream. But a sleeping dream is more vivid, more realistic. Psychotic or drug-induced hallucinations again use the same mechanism, but once more there is a difference of degree to the extent of increased reality tone.

Certain realities exist in the Astral — a point which can be proven experimentally. (See, among others, Israel Regardie's *Golden Dawn*.) But while these realities exist, they are *experienced* differently by individuals. That is, they take on varying forms in accordance with the psychological bias of the observer. This has a fairy-tale ring about it, but all that is meant is that a colour-blind man sees the world very differently from one with normal eyesight.

Let us assume for a moment that some form of Akashic Record exists on the Astral Plane. In other words, that an area of the Astral has a tendency to store impressions. Each of us has contact with the Astral via the imaginative faculty, so each of us, at least potentially, may explore the Plane and, in theory, reach the area of the Akashic. Does a theory of this nature show results in practice? The answer, once again, is a limited 'Yes.' Experienced astral travellers will often come in contact with an area of the Plane which behaves as the Akashic Record has always been reputed to behave. Their visions may differ widely in form but they manage, nevertheless, to extract information from them.

Direct Contact

It would be stepping completely beyond the scope of this book for me to try to turn you into an experienced astral traveller. But fortunately there exists a technique which, *in some cases,* will short-circuit the natural sequence and bring you into direct contact with the record. The technique is, in fact, an astral operation, having certain points in common with meditation practice. It is based partially on Cayce's experience, partially on the fact that the Book of Life is virtually an archetype in the West, and partially on the recognized (hence psychologically valid) truth that most of our information is gleaned from books.

Here again it should be emphasized that this technique will not work for everyone. But it will work, often exceptionally well, for most. The main difficulty, in my experience, has been simple lack of perseverance. The technique is far from easy, and stamina is a difficult characteristic to develop.

Reading the Akashic

If you were to wander accidentally into the Akashic Record on the Astral Plane, you would experience it in accordance with your bias — i.e. you get what you expect, not what you deserve.

The technique outlined here works the situation in reverse. By an act of imagination, you create an astral shell suitable for the forces of the Akashic Record to act through. And since proximity, on the Astral Plane, is an aspect of clarity, not distance, practice will enable you to blend the two.

Where the technique falls down completely is with the rare individual who does not find the suggested image suitable for the Akashic Record. The reason why I have gone to some pains to point this out is that you may, in such a case, substitute a more suitable personal image. But before you do, make sure you have the theory of the operation fully mastered.

The image you should use in your initial attempts is Cayce's image of the library. And the way to use it is this: Set aside a room, a time and a chair, exactly as you did for meditation. The only difference is the time, which should not exceed 10 minutes during daily attempts for the first two weeks; and should not exceed 15 minutes thereafter until you are so totally familiar with the *modus operandi* that you are competent to make your own rules.

Sit on the chair, go through the complete relaxation process and close your eyes. Next, visualize yourself walking down a corridor towards a door. For the first week, visualize no more than this. Build your picture strongly each day, filling in as much detail as possible, until that corridor is as familiar to you as a room in your home.

When your picture of the corridor is vivid — and in any case not earlier than the second week — picture yourself opening the door and entering a massive library. Spend at least two weeks, and preferably more, building up the detail of this library. See the volumes on the shelves.

Explore the vast space this library takes up. Note its multitude of sections, for it is a library which contains every scrap of information on everything that has ever happened, on everyone who has ever existed.

No Short-Cuts

This is the most important (although most laborious) part of the entire exercise, and should not under any circumstances be glossed over. Every minute, every day you spend improving your picture brings ultimate success closer. If you attempt short-cuts on the preparation, you need expect no results whatsoever.

There will come a day when you are finally satisfied that you have built the vision to the very best of your ability. When that day comes, keep building for another week, then see yourself walking to the section of the library which houses your life history. Search the shelves until you find the volume with your name on the cover. Take it down, open it and read your reincarnation history.

Even when you learn, through practice, to visualize words on the page, you will find that not all the information is fed to you in this way. As with so many of the methods given in this book, pictures of your past lives will arise.

For those with the patience to master it, this method is one of the safest and most valuable outlined. But it has one thing in common with all the others. It produces information which must be checked out by less esoteric means before it can be accepted.

CHAPTER TWELVE

TIME TRAVEL

In the modern view, time is no longer absolute, but
dependent on the relative motion of observers making
the time measurements. According to the theory of
relativity, time is but one aspect of a more general four-
dimensional space-time continuum, which is the arena
in which events occur in the universe. Time and space
are different aspects of this underlying four-dimensional
continuum. Frequently time is described as a fourth
dimension.

Academic American Encyclopedia

If consideration of the Akashic Record in our last section
called for a broad outline of the Astral Plane, the technique
given now calls for a little more detail.

Imagine for a moment a sea spreading over the entire
world, rather as air does now. This sea would, of course,
touch on everything that exists, and be affected by
everything that happens. But the picture in your mind at the

moment is three-dimensional. See if you can grasp the idea of the sea extending in four dimensions, the final one being time.

If you can manage this difficult trick, you will have a reasonably good picture of the Astral Plane. Even if you cannot, you are at least aware of one of its most important characteristics — the fact that it touches the past as well as the present. (There is some suggestion that it may touch the future as well, but that is beyond the scope of this book.)

As you imagined the Astral Sea, you were, as mentioned in the previous section, engaging in an astral operation. It follows then that part of you at least is in contact with the Astral Plane and able to influence it.

What is the nature of this part? The important clue is its ability to influence. This would seem to suggest that a part of you has a similar, or possibly even identical, essence to the essence of the Astral Plane.

Astral Body

Occultists, in fact, hold this as a truism and teach that the part of you which influences the astral is a subtle body — an astral body.

Just as I made no attempt to argue the dogma of reincarnation, I make no attempt to argue the dogma of subtle bodies, and for much the same reason. Where the astral body is concerned, direct experience is usually possible. The direct experience will come as part of the technique, but before outlining methods, further theoretical information will be useful.

The astral body is one of several subtle bodies which coincides with the physical, although on another dimension. The location of the astral body is purely a pseudo-location in the geographical sense, but must be accepted for practical purposes. (In the way that you accept yourself as existing somehow behind the bridge of your nose.)

Nightly, as the physical body relaxes and a variety of psychological functions sink into unconsciousness, the astral body detaches — although retaining a tenuous connection which is only severed on death — and wanders through areas of the Astral Plane. This experience you remember as dreaming.

Apart from this natural splitting away of the astral body, it is possible to detach it consciously under other circumstances and, with practice, use it as a vehicle of consciousness on both Physical and Astral Planes.

That's the theory. If it is correct, you will readily appreciate two things. By detaching the astral body, you can travel along the Astral Plane. And, since the Astral Plane extends along a fourth dimension, you can — at least in theory — engage in a type of time travel.

In practice, you will find this peculiar four-dimensional movement will help you pick up information about your previous incarnations.

Journey Into Time

The first step of your journey into time is shaking loose your astral body. This is by no means easy to do fully, but fortunately astral operations are seldom all or nothing affairs, so some result is virtually certain. As in so many other occult exercises, relaxation is an important key. The separation of the astral body occurs naturally when you are relaxed by sleep, and you will have a few worthwhile conscious results unless you achieve a high degree of relaxation first.

Needless to say the relaxation technique described earlier is what should be applied here. Make sure all your muscles are completely limp, and if difficulties are experienced during the exercise itself, mentally check that tension has not crept in again.

Having relaxed fully, begin loosening-up operations. There are a number of ways open to you, but all of them involve expert use of the imagination and hence may require practice before results show.

The traditional method of moving out on the Astral Plane is to build an imaginary body and transfer your consciousness to it. The building of the body is easy enough for anyone with even average visualization ability. But the transfer of consciousness is a knack, and as such can take years to grasp.

Less tricky is the method of imagining yourself sinking down and out of your physical body, drifting slowly upwards from it, or sinking, then moving sideways out of it. The major drawback with all these variations is that they will occasionally produce etheric rather than astral projection, and while this is very interesting to experience, it is not what is wanted for your present purposes.

Whichever method you choose, use it regularly until you can carry it out easily and without hesitation. When this has been achieved, add on stage two of the exercise.

The projection of the astral body is a letting go, rather than an effort. And though the 'letting go' may be difficult — since it runs contrary to a lifetime of habit — once achieved, the rest comes relatively easily.

It is this 'letting go' which forms stage two of the exercise outlined above. The technique described aimed towards creating a situation in which letting go is easier, but in the final analysis, the trick itself is largely a matter of trial and error.

If you should find it difficult to gain the knack (and chances are you will), the following exercise may prove even more helpful than that given earlier.

Lie with your eyes closed and begin to sense your inner self. In particular, try to sense the location of your central node of consciousness, the thing you think of as 'I'.

In almost all of you, this centre will be located in the head, probably just behind the bridge of the nose. It may have another location: some Celts, in particular, sense the location as an area around the solar plexus.

But where the centre is located is not important, just so long as you have a conscious awareness of its location.

Once you have located the centre, try to confine your awareness to it. This is comparatively easy, although your attention may wander a little until you have had some practice.

The next step may be a little more difficult. You must persuade the centre to move. Move it anywhere at first until you get the hang of it. Later move it first into your head — if it is not already there. Then move it to the back of your head.

At this stage you may feel as though you are losing your balance. But try to remember you are already lying down so there is no way you can actually fall. The sensation itself seldom becomes extreme, and soon passes away altogether.

To aid the process of this movement, it can sometimes be useful to imagine yourself standing within the vast cavern of your skull — but quite often this visualization is unnecessary.

Once you have successfully moved the centre to the back of your head, you will feel an unmistakable sensation of pressure at the rear of your skull. This sensation is far from subtle: it feels as though something physical was pressing quite firmly against the skull bone.

The next step is to 'feel' along the inside of your skull by further moving the centre of consciousness until you find an opening. The opening is not, of course, physical, otherwise your brains would be in a bad way; but openings do exist in the sense that there are areas of the skull where the centre of consciousness can most easily pass through.

When you succeed in passing through, you may find yourself staring at the back of your own head; or sometimes looking down at yourself through a type of tunnel or tube.

Quite often, the surprise engendered by this abrupt change of viewpoint will send you scuttling straight back in again. But with practice, you will find you can come out and stay out.

Overall, the most helpful analogy to the release process of the astral body is the physical act of urination. Forcing the bladder to function is quite useless, as many patients discover when their doctor requires a urine sample. Indeed, the harder you try, the more difficult it is to comply. What is needed, as a fact of everyday experience, is a very specific relaxation, which allows nature to take its course. A similar relaxation, part physical, part mental, will permit supernature (to borrow Lyall Watson's useful term) to take its course in releasing the astral body.

Once released from your body, there is an excellent chance other things will fall into place quite naturally — because the Astral Plane is the natural functional environment of the astral body. It seems that the Astral Plane lies in a particular 'direction', but a 'direction' impossible to sense while still linked with the physical vehicle. Once out of the body, however, an appreciable number of projectors can 'turn in the right direction' quite easily and enter the Astral Plane as automatically as a cyclist balances a bicycle.

I have been liberal in my use of quotation marks around words like 'direction', but this is purely to show special usage when considered from our usual physical viewpoint. Make no mistake about it: once out of the body, terms like 'direction' may be taken quite literally because they are used to describe your own subjective sensation of what is happening to you.

Once you reach the Astral Plane in full consciousness — as opposed to the form of imaginative contact described earlier — you will find yourself in an intriguing environment.

Paradoxically, your first impression may well be one of utter normality. There is a sky overhead, and the ground beneath your feet is firm. There may well be familiar, earth-type sights — plants, flowers, trees, rocks, even buildings. But you may possibly find you are dressed differently to the way you were before projection; and you will certainly find you can fly, at will, like Superman.

Even more disturbing is the fact that you can think things into existence. One colleague of mine, making her third journey to the Astral, created a perfect rose bush and reported back that artifacts of this type, while solid and three dimensional, had a curious hint of 'sharpness' about them, like something added to a painting at a later date.

Several experimenters, aided a little by hypnotic suggestion, have been able to find their way to a pre-existent Akashic Record while exploring the Astral Plane. This structure — if that is the word — formed part of a Temple building and required no visualization to call it into being. Once again it was in the form of a library, but with the added utility of a large viewing screen on which pictures of past lives might be projected.

While all of this must seem fanciful, ridiculous or outlandish to readers lacking esoteric experience, the existence and form of the Astral Plane is an empirical fact, attested to by countless psychics, projectors and occultists. If, in your own experiments, you reach this odd level, the few words of description given here may prove very useful to you indeed.

CHAPTER THIRTEEN

REMINDERS OF
THE PAST

It is ... clear that humans have long-term memory for
sensory information — for the sound of a violin, the
taste of an apple, or the color of a sunset. Such
information is stored in some relatively permanent
form; whether different sensory modalities are stored
separately, or whether they form part of a more
general memory store, is at present unclear.

Academic American Encyclopedia

Not all techniques aimed at the recall of past lives are as
weird as those we have so far been examining. The secret
of almost all reincarnation research is that the memories of
your past lives actually exist, here and now, in some deep
stratum of your unconscious mind. The trick is to recall
them; and recall of memories is something we do all the
time.

But for something we do all the time — and could
scarcely survive without doing — the use of memory is very

poorly understood by the average individual ... which may explain why the average individual has recall so poor as to be shameful were it not for the fact that most other people can do little better.

Almost everyone memorizes in the same way. If there is something we wish to remember — a poem, a phone number, a shopping list — we repeat it again and again in the hope that it might eventually 'sink' in. Sometimes the technique even succeeds, but at the cost of enormous effort and in a manner so erratic that memory itself seems fundamentally unreliable.

But memory is not fundamentally unreliable. All that happens here is that we use memory in a very inefficient way. You can test this for yourself. Have a look at this list of 25 randomly selected items culled from a memory-training book I once wrote for young readers:

Typewriter
Snake
Washing machine
Teddy bear
Bronze statue
Cactus
Painting
Egyptian mummy
Persian rug
Egg-cup
Dictionary
Can of cola
Telephone
Horse
Notebook
Ship in a bottle
Walking stick

Plate of egg and chips
Elephant
Potted palm
Guitar
Pair of boots
Motor car
Vampire bat
Pound of butter

To memorize that list would, I suspect, take quite a lot of effort. But I would like you to apply that effort over, say, the next five minutes and learn the list as best you can.

Having done so, I want you to leave this book aside, go off and do something interesting for half an hour. What you do is your choice — watch television, make yourself a snack, jog, whatever. When the half hour is up, take a pen and piece of paper and list down as many of the items as you can remember. If you get even half right, you will be doing very well indeed.

But your poor performance is not indicative of a bad memory (as you might be excused for thinking). It is only indicative of a badly-*used* memory. If you care to spend the next five minutes memorizing the list in a slightly different way, you will be pleasantly surprised by the result.

The Memory Locus

Imagine your own home. By 'imagine' I mean make a picture in your mind. Visualize your home the way you might do if you were daydreaming. For the next few minutes, your home is going to be your *locus*, the place where you put things you want to remember.

Imagine yourself standing outside your own front door. Try to visualize it as vividly as possible, noting the colour of the paint, the shine on the brass knocker and so on. Imagine a gigantic typewriter — the first item on your list — blocking the door so that you can scarcely squeeze through. Imagine yourself clambering over the typewriter to reach the knocker or the bell-push. But as you use this, it turns into a snake — item 2 — in your hand, so you have to throw it away in panic in case it bites you.

The door is swinging open now and you are stepping into your hallway ... where a big white washing machine is chugging merrily away, spewing suds in a flood that threatens to ruin your hall carpet.

And so on. Go through your home and your list until you have placed all 25 items, finishing with the pound of butter. Do not waste time on any one: just visualize it as clearly as you can, put it in place, and imagine yourself going on to the next room, corridor or whatever. You can put two or more items in the same room if you think you might be running out of space.

There are several ways to get the best from this technique. One is to exaggerate the size of each item, unless it happens to be pretty big to begin with. When I started out, for instance, I imagined a really massive typewriter at the front door.

Make your mental pictures dramatic, if the situation permits, as we did with the washing machine which was flooding the front hall. Finally, make some, all or most of your mental pictures ludicrous, amusing or silly.

Now comes the moment of truth. Put the list away, take a pen and paper, imagine yourself at the front door of your house and write down 'typewriter', since that is what you can see there. Climb over the typewriter, reach for the knocker which changes into a snake. Throw the snake aside before it strikes you, then write down 'snake'. Take the same route through your home as you did before, and write down the various items as you find them in the rooms you visit. Do not worry if you draw an occasional blank. Just keep going to the next room and write down what you find there. When you've finished, check your score.

You may actually have all 25 items correct (and in the correct order as well), but even if you have not, chances are you will have done far better using this simple visualization technique than you did trying to learn the items off by heart the old way. This is simply because you are using your memory more efficiently than usual.

We learn to think in words at such an early age that we tend to forget verbal skills are actually quite alien to the human mind. Left to its own devices, your mind works most comfortably in filing away experiences in their entirety rather than just their verbal description.

Chain of Associations

The various elements of these experiences — visual, audible, tactile etc — form a chain of associations leading back to the totality of the experience itself. This is why, in the famous fictional passage, Proust's hero suddenly finds himself experiencing a vivid visionary memory of his childhood triggered by the *taste* of a madeleine biscuit dipped in a cup of tea.

The mechanics of far memory — memories of past life experiences — are no different to the mechanics of normal memory. Far memory works by association — linking visual, audible, tactile and olfactory elements back to the totality of the experience. Once you realize this, it is a short step towards setting up an interesting do-it-yourself programme designed to stimulate far memory.

For this you will need to make a (smallish) financial investment and call on the assistance of a friend.

In preparation for your programme you will need to obtain the following items:

1. A *pictorial* reference source of antique furniture. *Lyall's Antique Guide,* which is updated annually to give current antique prices, is ideal, but there are other similar sources if you have difficulty finding this one. Inquire at your favourite bookshop.
2. A selection of historical music, preferably recorded using authentic instrumentation of the times. The Past Times shops (in London, Exeter, Cambridge, Oxford, Chichester and York) carry a small but extremely useful collection of cassettes ranging from the popular songs of the First World War to the music of ancient Greece.

When you have acquired these items, take care that you do *not* examine them: pass them directly on to the friend who has agreed to help you in establishing your programme.

Your friend should then prepare your programme for you by a) selecting a series of pictures in the antique reference which cover as broad an historical timespan as possible. It is permissible to include items other than furniture in order to extend the range, but have your friend concentrate on furniture where possible, and b) organizing the running order of a musical session for you to listen to. The session should consist of a mixum-gatherum of the material you have collected, with no attempt made to follow any historical time sequence. (Indeed, care should be taken to go for a *random* pattern, so that a Tudor piece might be followed by a lute recital from ancient Rome, and so on.)

When these extensive preparations are complete, equip yourself with a notebook and pen, set aside an afternoon for the experiment and proceed as follows:

Relax as deeply as possible. You might even like to go through the relaxation sequence given earlier (see Chapter 8). Once you are comfortable and relaxed, have your friend show you, one at a time, the antique furniture pictures he or she has selected. Care should be taken at this stage that you have no indication of the period to which the picture belongs. (Any captions of headings which would give the game away should be covered or blacked out.)

Emotional Reactions

As you view each one, make a note of your emotional reaction to it. Decide whether you like it, dislike it, or are completely neutral towards it. Try to visualize the item in its natural surroundings and imagine yourself in those surroundings too. Watch out for any mental pictures that might spontaneously arise, and note their details.

When you have finished examining the selection of pictures, move on to your music session. Lie back in your relaxed state and listen while your friend plays the selection of music. Each piece need not be long — indeed no more than a minute or two will be enough for the experiment and will permit a wider range of music to be heard in a given time. As each piece finishes, your friend should pause to allow you to make a note of any emotions generated by the music and, more particularly, any mental pictures which arose while you were listening to it. As with the pictures, note whether you liked, disliked or were neutral about each piece.

Your friend should not make any comment until after the complete session (pictures and music) has ended. At this stage, however, you can get together to analyse the results.

First, weed out those pictures and musical pieces to which you had a neutral emotional reaction. They will play no further part in the experiment. Next, examine those you particularly liked, checking back with your friend to see if there is any connection between them — for example originating in the same country, or from the same historical period. Do the same for those items you particularly disliked, again checking for any common denominator.

Finally, check through your notes of the mental images which arose during the experiment and check to find out if these relate accurately to the picture or musical selection which stimulated them.

What you are looking for are indications of any particular attraction to, or repulsion from, a particular historical period. If you find evidence of either, there is a chance (and no more than a chance at this stage) that the period concerned was one in which you lived before.

The analysis of the mental images may prove the most rewarding, for it is here that you may generate hard evidence of past life recall. (Up to this point, everything has been merely an *indication* of direction and nothing more.) As a working hypothesis, treat the images exactly as if they were indeed far memories generated by techniques like hypnosis.

Try to put yourself into those scenes which correlate accurately with the historical period of the picture or music that prompted them. Look for incidental detail which you can check later against historical sources. Above all, avoid the mistake of assuming it is all 'just imagination'. The time to decide how much is imagination and how much genuine far memory is *after* you have checked historical records.

CHAPTER FOURTEEN

NOTES FOR SERIOUS STUDENTS

The most serious problem that parapsychology has in gaining full recognition as a legitimate science, is the inability of nonparapsychologists to duplicate their findings. Some parapsychologists realize that they must first find ways to reliably produce psi phenomena before they can seriously demand attention. A phenomenon that occurs only for a select group of observers — and then only unpredictably and in contradictory ways — violates all the rules of objectivity necessary for scientific investigation.

Academic American Encyclopedia.

You can approach reincarnation research in one of two ways. You can treat it as a game, a bit of a giggle to liven up a party, a light-hearted romp that might give you something to talk about when you have finished with football. Or you can take it seriously, as something worth doing carefully and conscientiously for the sake of increased knowledge, wisdom and insight. I confess a bias towards the latter approach. But even so, I can't help feeling the former has its points. The danger of obsession is as pronounced in reincarnation research as it is in any branch of esotericism. And the best antidote to obsession is a healthy sense of humour.

What a pity so many occultists take themselves so seriously! Their work may have its life and death aspects, but so does the work of an engine driver or a steeplejack. Heaven knows how many thousand potential students have been lost to occultism through the doleful faces and sepulchral voices of its practitioners.

But with that reservation, a serious approach seems to me to be the only one worth following. Things being what they are, it is an approach with responsibilities.

Psychical research is virtually the only field of human investigation where the amateur still has some chance of competing with the professional. The days of the spare-time research chemist or physicist are gone for good. But the person who decides to investigate the outlandish realms of parapsychology may still discover a thing or two before the scientist does.

Changing Situation

The situation is not, however, static. At the turn of the century, virtually the only people investigating telepathy were amateurs. The same was true for precognition, clairvoyance and telekinesis. Today, these areas are almost exclusively the preserve of scientists and statisticians, with new facts and theories likely to emerge only from the laboratory.

As conservatism breaks down and less and less is taken for granted (or dismissed), science is looking more and more towards occult curios. Reincarnation, as an hypothesis, will eventually be put through the mill — with what result remains to be seen. But until that day comes, reincarnation investigators are in much the same position as the founders of the Society for Psychical Research. It is possibly not too much to hope that they will acquit themselves as well as their Victorian counterparts.

What all this is leading up to is a plea based on the notion that if something is worth doing at all, it is worth doing properly.

In this handbook, you have been given a number of methods which, properly used, can be exceptional tools for insight into your past lives. Since no single method works for everyone, the techniques were purposely varied to ensure that the best possible chance exists for you to find at least one which works for you. And when you do, it could be well worth while following the example of the early psychical investigators and keeping careful records both of your original experiments and the subsequent checking-out procedures.

Record Keeping

All the techniques given are such as to require a note taken of results at the time of the experiment. This is expecially true of the methods designed to produce visions. Information dredged from the unconscious has a peculiar habit of evaporating into thin air with astounding speed. It is like trying to capture a dream. You wake up with vivid memories of the fantastic time you were having, turn over or get out of bed, and suddenly ... what *was* that dream? or did I dream at all? The sensation of forgetting visionary information is so similar that I suspect the same psychological mechanism is involved. The cure is simple: a note taken at the time.

If you happen to own a tape recorder, you have at your fingertips the greatest aid to note-taking since shorthand. Although some occultists seem to have a built-in aversion to the products of modern technology, a recorder is invaluable for this type of work. With it, you can use almost any of the techniques without having to call on outside assistance. And the record of your experience will be totally accurate ... in *every* detail. (The point is less obvious than it may appear: human note-takers have a tendency to censor details which seem irrelevant or mistaken. Sometimes these are the very details which provide the strongest evidence later.)

But if you don't have a recorder — and can't borrow one — pen and paper will suffice. In some of the experiments, you will not be able to make notes yourself, (under hypnosis, for example), so arrange for the help of a sympathetic friend. The adjective is carefully chosen. There is nothing more inhibiting than trying to carry out occult experiments watched by a cynic. And apart from its inherent discomfort, inhibition frequently upsets the delicate mental processes you are attempting to set in motion, so that results become increasingly difficult to obtain.

Layout Example

Take notes exactly as they come and transcribe them in the same way. Afterwards, break your notes down into a standard sequence. This will make them easier to evaluate and compare.

An example follows.

Environment	Description	Detail	Comment
	Open plain.	Distant lake with mountain beyond, possibly volcanic. Strong sun.	Sensation of familiarity.
Place	No direct information.	–	Certainly tropical. Possibly Africa.
Time	No direct information.	–	Impossible to guess.
Own appearance	Primitive. Dark skin.	Tribal costume and body paint. Bone spear and club.	Aware I was a hunter and warrior.
Company	Seven men.	Similar dress and weapons.	
Developments	None.	Fleeting vision.	

Overall Comment:	Self-evidently, this one will be quite impossible to check out in any scientific manner. File under possible African incarnation and hope later experiments will throw some light on it.
Technique:	Astral travel.
Date:	13 November 1989.

Retain Notes

File this shortened account of your vision along with the transcribed notes *and the original notes themselves*. This latter point is important since at any time you may hit on highly evidential material where it will be important to rule out the possibility of error in transcription.

Whether you experiment for a series of visions, or check out each one as you go along, is largely a matter of taste.

But as I have said so often in this book, a check-up must be made unless your experiments are to degenerate into a series of parlour games.

Human nature being what it is, your hopes will be that the check will prove your visions valid. But never get disheartened if the opposite occurs. It is far better to have a hundred visions proved wrong than to cling to one romantic notion of a past life which might be sheer fantasy.

When you do begin to investigate the factual basis of your visions, record keeping is just as vital as when you were experimenting with the visions themselves. Ask for information in writing where possible. If you have to accept verbal information, take a written note of it at the time, or as soon afterwards as humanly possible. *Never, never trust to memory.* I was once a newspaper reporter and I can assure you that the only thing relying on memory ever does is get you into trouble.

As you broke down your visions for easy reference, it is a good idea to break down check-up evidence in the same way:

Source	Date(s)	Details	Comment
Alantown Parish Register	1870 August 1st	Birth of John Foster.	Would tie in approx. with age of Foster in vision of 4/1/90.
Rev. Smyth	circa 1930	Recalls Foster as an old man. Birthmark still in evidence.	Birthmark vital evidence.

Overall Comment:	This fits in exceptionally well with the vision of 4/1/90 and would certainly warrant further investigation.
Date:	30 January 1990.

PECULIARITIES OF REINCARNATION

Exorcism is the ritual act of expelling demons, or evil
spirits, from persons or other creatures. The practice
has its roots in primitive religions and was taken over
by Judaism and Christianity. Traditionally, various
levels of demonic possession have been believed to
occur, and the rites of exorcism have varied
accordingly.

Academic American Encyclopedia

As you set out to investigate your past lives — and
especially if you do so seriously, with dedication — there is
little doubt that you will uncover information that will
deepen your self-knowledge and expand your personal
philosophy.

But there is also a chance that you will uncover
peculiarities which can be emotionally disturbing if you are
unprepared for them. Throughout this book, I have tried to
emphasize that reincarnation is almost certainly not what

most people imagine it to be. The process of rebirth, if it has any reality at all, is more complicated and peculiar than its popular image.

Just how peculiar is illustrated by the two brief case histories that follow.

Two Mystery Cases

Mary Roff, a young American girl with a history of epilepsy, died in Peoria, Illinois, in 1865. In 1877, Lurancy Vennum, the teenage daughter of an Illinois farmer, underwent two nights of visions, followed, a week later, by a five-hour trance.

Trances became a daily occurrence for several months, and severe abdominal pains occurred. In January 1878 the personality of Lurancy Vennum changed to that of Mary Roff. The change was striking. Not only did Lurancy think she was Mary Roff, but she was also aware of intimate details of the dead girl's life.

Mary Roff's parents were convinced. On 11 February, with the agreement of all parties concerned, Lurancy/Mary went to live with the Roffs. The secondary personality continued to manifest until near the end of May, when it disappeared for good.

There is a volume of documentary evidence on this curious case, since it attracted considerable attention at the time both from the world of science and the press. Details of the case point strongly to the fact that the secondary personality was indeed that of Mary Roff.

But was it a case of reincarnation? Certainly not in the usual sense of the word, since Lurancy was already 15 months old when Mary died.

Collapsed

Crossing a bridge over the Corace river near Siano, Italy, in 1939, 17-year-old Maria Talarico collapsed. She was carried home to bed, where she went into convulsions. When the convulsions ended, Maria's former personality had vanished. Now she was manifesting the personality of a young man named Guiseppe (Pepe) Veraldi.

A note written by her later proved to be in handwriting identical to that of the youth who had died, in rather mysterious circumstances, at the age of 19 in 1936.

She recognized a photograph of a sister of Veraldi's whom Maria had never known, she recognized Veraldi's brothers, she recognized a photograph of a friend's sister, she recognized a Customs official Veraldi had known ... and she claimed that as Veraldi she had been murdered.

Again reincarnation of a sort. Again not the sort of reincarnation particularly familiar to students of the esoteric. The usual label on a case such as that of Maria Talarico is 'possession'. But when the invading personality is that of an individual who died previously, the mechanics of the situation seem very close to those of reincarnation.

That is, of course, assuming we will ever understand the mechanics of either ...

INDEX